Meet Me
in the
Valley

Walking with God
through the
low places in life

Meet Me
in the
Valley

Walking with God
through the
low places in life

KATHY R. GREEN

REDEMPTION
PRESS

Meet Me in the Valley, by Kathy R. Green

Published by Redemption Press
PO Box 427
Enumclaw, WA 98022
Toll free (844-2REDEEM [273-3336])

Unless otherwise noted, all Scripture quotations are taken from the *Holy Bible*, New Living Translation, copyright © 1996, 2004, 2007 by Tyndale House Foundation. Used by permission of Tyndale House Publishers, Inc., Carol Stream, Illinois 60188. All rights reserved.

Scripture quotations marked AMPC are taken from the Amplified Bible® Classic Edition, copyright © 1954, 1958, 1962, 1964, 1965, 1987 by The Lockman Foundation. Used by permission of The Lockman Foundation, La Habra, CA 90631. All rights reserved. www.Lockman.org.

Scripture quotations marked NKJV are taken from the New King James Version. Copyright © 1982. Thomas Nelson. All rights reserved. Used by permission.

Cover design by Bill Johnson
Digg Design Studio

Library of Congress Control Number: 2018958381

ISBN: 978-1-68314-205-8
        978-1-68314-206-5 (hardcover)
        978-1-68314-207-2 (epub)
        978-1-68314-208-9 (mobi)

First Edition
Printed in the United States

Dedication

To my beautiful mother, Rosie. Thank you for showing me how to stand strong and weather the storms of life. I honor you and love you with all my heart.

Acknowledgments

To my husband, Cliff: Thank you for being so loving, kind, and patient toward me and allowing me the freedom to passionately pursue and obey God's call on my life. Your unwavering support sure makes my life much easier.

To my children: Emonne, Stephan, Jordan, Myra, thank you for all your love, help, and support. Each of you inspires me in a special way.

To my grandchildren: Grace and Josiah, you fill my life with joy. Thank you for sharing your nana with the others.

To my pray-ers: Thank you for covering me while writing this book. I could not have accomplished this mission without your fervent prayers.

To the team at Redemption Press: Athena, Inger, Serena, Dori, Jeanette, Hannah, CJ, and Rachel. Thank you for helping me birth this baby in excellence.

CONTENTS

Even when I walk through the darkest valley, I will not be afraid, for you are close beside me. ~Psalm 23:4

Introduction

Meet Me in the Valley.

When the Lord spoke those words to my heart, I was in the midst of one of the most difficult seasons of my life. If I was willing to go into a deeper realm of intimacy with Him, I knew I would experience God afresh.

The very thought of this intrigued me, but there were things I needed to learn and experience before He would allow me to move further into my destiny.

I met God in that valley, and the lessons learned through that experience brought forth the rich insights I share in this book.

The greatest treasures of wisdom and knowledge are not unearthed during our mountaintop experiences; they are found in the deepest valleys, when we walk hand in hand with the Lord. As much as we would rather avoid the kind of circumstances that take us to a low place, these experiences are essential for our spiritual growth and development. They prepare us for the work to which we are called.

Are you currently facing a situation that seems beyond recovery or impossible to bear? Despite how good and obedient we may be, none of us are exempt from trouble. God allows us to endure tests and trials for a higher purpose, but it's up to each of us to recognize and accept these divine opportunities and glean all we possibly can from them. There are valuable lessons to be learned and great rewards to be gained by walking through life's most difficult circumstances. Valleys are rich with discoveries about God and ourselves.

A few years ago, during a time of prayer, I received a vision from the Lord. Before me, two enormous mountains stood side by side, with their bases touching. The mountains blocked my way and kept me from moving forward and making progress on my journey. As I pondered what to do, the mountains suddenly shifted, one to the right and the other to the left. A road appeared between them.

I stopped to consider how God handled my situation. He could have lifted me up over the mountaintops, but He didn't. He could have given me the strength and ability to climb the mountains, but He didn't. Nor did He tell me to speak to the mountains and command them to move out of my way. Instead, God moved them aside and revealed a pathway for me to walk between them, and then, in the midst of that valley, created an overwhelming desire within me to venture onward and see what awaited me on the other side.

Despite how impossible a situation may appear, God has a plan to get us through it. Only by determining to walk through whatever life brings our way can we become who God has destined us to be and do what He has called us to do.

It takes faith to stare mountains of impossibility in the face and still be convinced that God can and will get us safely to the other side.

When we face seasons of hardship and trouble, may we adopt the desire to meet God and walk close beside Him.

My mission and reason for writing this book is not to glorify suffering or make light of life's difficulties. I'm here to encourage you not to grow weary when you encounter trouble. I want to help you to see things from a higher perspective. Throughout this book I will share some of the valuable insights I gained during the most difficult times of my life, including the four-year valley that resulted in this book.

Each experience, one building upon the next, culminated in knowing God more intimately. Through this book, I hope to offer you a fresh outlook on how God utilizes the lowest points in our lives for His glory.

I've discovered that the true beauty of journeying through a valley is the ascent up the hill of the Lord. Walking through low places provides the opportunity for deep conversations with our Creator, the Lover of our souls, along the way.

You may choose to read through this book chapter by chapter at your own pace, or as twenty-one daily devotional readings. However you approach the words of this book, I pray God will illumine your heart and mind, allowing you to see your life from a higher point of view: His. God wants to lead you through this time in your life, and every difficult situation you will ever encounter, guiding you by the hand each step of the journey.

As He leads you into your God-appointed destiny, may you discover new things about God, life, and yourself . . . simply because you had the courage to meet Him in the valley.

Chapter 1

THE JOURNEY

Whenever I drive to a place I've never been, I always seem to get turned around. I am directionally challenged, and I have never been able to follow a map. But with the aid of my cell phone, the navigation system in my car, and a few landmarks to spot along the way, I always arrive at my destination.

This journey called *life* is much like traveling to a place we've never been. Even if we know our exact locations today, and hopefully we have a good sense of where we are going, challenges still remain in what we encounter along the journey. None of us knows what's coming around the corner. The unexpected and unforeseeable valleys of life can leave us feeling disoriented, as if we've lost our way.

Even when we face valleys that rock us to the core and push our faith to the limit, God is still with us.

One thing that helps me endure difficult seasons is being aware of the big picture. Keeping the vision before me, that big-picture view which speaks of the future—the place God is calling me to. When I take a step back and look at life from a broader point of view, I can assess where I am on the road to my destiny: the preordained place where I fulfill my kingdom assignment and impact those I am called to reach for His glory. Reflecting on the vision helps to remind me of who I am in Christ, and my relationship with God, and His promises to me.

Six Stages of Our Christian Walk

As Christians, our real journey begins on the day we accept Jesus as our Lord and Savior. Although God promised to never leave us or forsake us, He never promised us a life of ease and continuous pleasure.

The Twenty-Third Psalm offers us a real picture of our life's journey, in light of our relationship with God as Father, Son, and Spirit. Each verse reveals a different stage we encounter as followers of Christ. It's one thing to read the eloquent words penned by the psalmist David, or even recite them by memory, but what's even better is to have a revelation about what David is trying to convey. If we fully grasp the heart of the message, it will help make our journey much easier to bear.

Let us take a closer look at what I refer to as "The Six Stages of Our Christian Walk," based on the six verses in Psalm 23, to gain a better understanding of the different seasons God allows us to walk through and what we discover along the way. You will notice how our journey takes on a variety of forms as we confront life's circumstances.

When we are faced with trouble, our first instinct is often to turn to someone for care and comfort. But even loved ones and close friends with the best intentions lack the capacity to meet our greatest needs and the inner longings of our hearts. But God is the Great Shepherd who cares for His sheep exactly the way we need to be cared for. When we're in the midst of trouble, we must look to God above all else.

1. **Knowing God as Shepherd**

> The Lord is my Shepherd [to feed, guide, and
> shield me], I shall not lack.
> ~Psalm 23:1 AMPC

In the first stage of our journey, we come to know God as our Father. This should be the basis and foundation of our relationship with Him. We recognize Jesus as God's Son, our Savior and Lord who gave His life for us, that He is alive and seated at the right hand of God, interceding for us each day. We know the Holy Spirit came to earth in Jesus's place, and that He is in us and with us as Comforter, Counselor, Standby, Strengthener, Advocate, and Revealer of Truth. When we first give our lives to the Lord, we begin to learn and grow in our understanding of who God (Father, Son, and Spirit) is through daily fellowship, spending time in the Word, and prayer.

In this stage of our journey, we discover that God is the true source of our supply. He meets all our needs. He cares for us. He feeds us and sustains us. In our immaturity, we struggle to find nourishment and strength elsewhere until we arrive at the point of knowing God as our Shepherd.

David came to know the Lord while spending time in the fields, tending his father's flock. In the stillness of time spent alone with God, he learned how to guide the sheep, provide for their daily needs, and keep them safe from harm. David's experiences taught him to declare the Lord as his Shepherd because he understood the unique 'relationship between a shepherd and his sheep. From this deep revelation, he penned one of the most famous passages ever written in Scripture. The Twenty-Third Psalm brings comfort to our hearts in times of trouble.

Like David, we must also come to know the Lord and to declare Him to be our Shepherd. He will take great care of us and provide for our every need.

2. **Learning to Rest in Him**

> He makes me lie down in [fresh, tender] green pastures; He leads me beside the still and restful waters. ~Psalm 23:2 AMPC

In the second stage of our journey, we learn how to rest in God's peace. The green pastures represent life and how God nourishes us. The calm waters are symbolic of the calmness He wants us to experience from the inside out as we cease from fretting, worrying, and being anxious about the circumstances and cares of this world. We can live a carefree life when we allow God to care for us.

In this place of rest, we practice how to quietly wait in God's presence despite our outward struggles and inner turmoil. God allows us to stay here as long as necessary, and He determines when it's time for us to move on. Where can we better find quietness and rest for our souls than in God's presence? Too often, we struggle to enter into rest. But by the time we do, we have reached a certain level of spiritual maturity. God can then lead us on to the next phase of our journey.

3. **Being Healed and Restored in His Presence**

> He refreshes *and* restores my life (my self);
> He leads me in the paths of righteousness
> [uprightness and right standing with Him—
> not for my earning it, but] for His name's
> sake. ~Psalm 23:3 AMPC

As we rest in the third stage of our journey, God comforts our hurting hearts and heals the emotional wounds we carry. He restores our minds, frees us of mental torment, and stabilizes and strengthens us emotionally. As we allow God to heal and restore us to wholeness of mind and heart, He can then lead us down the paths of righteousness that He has paved specifically for us. He leads us further along the journey to destiny, into what He has called us to do.

4. **Trusting in Him**

> Yes, though I walk through the [deep, sunless] valley of the shadow of death, I will fear *or* dread no evil, for You are with me; Your rod [to protect] and Your staff [to guide], they comfort me. ~Psalm 23:4 AMPC

In this fourth stage of our journey, even with the Lord leading us, we still encounter valleys. Remember, valleys are inevitable as long as we are on the earth. These paths may appear dark and hopeless, but because the Lord walks close beside us, we don't have to fear what will happen. This is what this book is all about—to help you grow in your knowledge of God and successfully walk through difficult places in life.

Despite how long or trying your journey may be, it is only a shadow, appearing as something more than it really is. Nothing can harm you or change who you are in Christ. Nothing can keep you from your God-appointed destiny.

As long as God is with us, we have no reason to fear. His rod protects us from our adversary. His shepherd's staff guides us along our journey as the Holy Spirit comforts our hearts every step of the way.

One day we will no longer be on earth where life is tough, where the Enemy comes to steal from, kill, and destroy the people of God. We will be in the presence of God for all eternity.

5. Receiving God's Blessings and Rewards

> You prepare a table before me in the presence
> of my enemies. You anoint my head with oil;
> my [brimming] cup runs over. ~Psalm 23:5
> AMPC

In the fifth stage of the journey, God rewards us for our suffering. It's as if He prepares a beautifully decorated table with the most delicious spread of our favorite things and then sits us down and anoints us with the oil of gladness.

By the time we arrive at this point in our Christian walk, we will have gone through our share of tests and trials and come through victoriously. Our enemy, Satan, as well as any earthly enemies who have warred against us become mere spectators to what the Lord does for us, watching from a distance, unable to partake of—or interfere with—what God has prepared for us to enjoy.

As God anoints us with the oil of gladness, He fills our cup with His goodness until it overflows and we become a blessing to others. Won't it be wonderful to be seated at the Lord's table? If we stand strong and refuse to give up, we will get there. All we need to do is keep walking hand in hand with Him along the journey.

6. Walking in Victory

Surely *or* only goodness, mercy, *and* unfailing love shall follow me all the days of my life, and through the length of my days the house of the Lord [and His presence] shall be my dwelling place. ~Psalm 23:6 AMPC

In the sixth and final stage of our journey, we are convinced that God is a good and loving Father. We experience the goodness of the Lord in the land of the living. His mercy follows us everywhere we go. No matter what, come what may, we are determined to stay close to God and to spend the rest of our days in the presence of the Lord, here on earth and throughout eternity.

Now that you've had a chance to examine the Christian walk in six stages, where do you see yourself on the journey? Do you need to learn to rest in God, or trust Him more? Are you convinced of His faithfulness and ability to care for you?

- **Point to ponder: Despite what we encounter along life's journey, God is there to feed, guide, and protect us along the way.**

Let's pray together before moving on to the next chapter.

Lord, teach me how to walk with You the way David did, the man after Your own heart. I want to know You as my Great Shepherd. I want to learn how to rest and relax in Your presence as I surrender to Your perfect will for my life. Please restore my mind, will, and emotions from the events of my past and the things that have wounded my heart. I refuse to fear, because I know You are with me. Help me to rise above every situation I encounter until I am seated at Your table. Please anoint me with the oil of Your Spirit until my cup overflows with blessings. I want to live in Your abiding presence forever and ever. In Jesus's name I pray. Amen!

Chapter 2

LIFE'S VALLEYS

I love to observe the magnificent landscape of God's creation. When our children were little, my husband and I moved to Southern California. What a wonderful and gorgeous place to live. Although we were only there for a few years, it remains at the top of my list of favorite places to live. Despite its beauty, the Pacific Ocean wasn't what took my breath away. It was the mysteriousness of the mountains that I couldn't seem to get enough of. I'm not sure where my fascination with mountains came from, but I could gaze at them all day long.

One day we took a drive on a winding two-lane road near our home. Rounding a bend in the road, I gasped. Right there before me, big and beautiful, lush and green, and so close I could almost reach out my hand and touch them . . .

Mountains.

If only I'd had wings, I would have flown all around them.

The mountains were something beautiful we did not expect to encounter on our journey. As we continued on our drive, we eventually ended up in the historic little town of Fillmore.

A small agricultural city with a population of around seventeen thousand people, Fillmore, California, sat at the foot of those mountains. It was cute, quaint, and rich with history, but there was nothing spectacular about it. Compared to our earlier view, it didn't seem like much. I'm sure if we had stayed in that valley long enough to explore, there would have been wonderful things to discover, but we turned around and began to ascend back up to the mountains that had taken our breath away.

To appreciate the beauty of every mountain, we must be willing to visit a few valleys.

Mountains and valleys go hand in hand. Both are necessary to gain a true-to-life portrait of our human experience. Life is a journey filled with highs and lows, ups and downs. Experiencing different altitudes and elevations is what challenges us to continue to learn and grow. It makes life interesting instead of boring, adventurous instead of dull, enlightening instead of uninformative, and balanced instead of grossly unbalanced.

A mountaintop provides a panoramic view of life, making everything around us look more beautiful. We may even feel as if we can conquer the world. But from a valley standpoint, surrounded by mountains that appear as walls of impossibility, leaving us wondering how we will ever get through them, life can look dark and hopeless.

Literally speaking, a valley is an area of low land between hills or mountains. Figuratively speaking, however, a valley can be defined as a divinely ordained place of God-discovery and self-discovery. In fact, we can view life's valleys as God's classroom because of the rich insights and invaluable wisdom and knowledge to be gained by walking through them.

Valleys Are Symbolic

Valleys symbolize our lowest points in life. They represent our darkest hours and our greatest tests, the times we find ourselves facing trouble as a result of an unfortunate and unexpected life event. It could be the loss of a loved one, job, or personal property. A life-threatening illness or other physical condition. Or perhaps a failed relationship or financial disaster. Valleys are not a representation of the typical challenges we face as a normal part of daily life. They represent the most difficult situations we encounter, and they are distinctive points on our journey.

Valleys Are Transitional

Valleys are passageways from one point in our lives to the next. We are not where we used to be, nor have we arrived at the place we were destined for. We are somewhere between.

Valleys are never intended to be a permanent dwelling place or a final destination. They only exist to teach us what we need to know so that we can be promoted to our next level. Often, our attitude plays a significant role in the length of our stay in a valley. The more we yield to the process and allow God to have His way, the sooner He can lead us out of the valley and into brighter days.

Valleys Are Solitary

Valleys are often accompanied by feelings of loneliness and isolation, but every experience is unique to the individual walking through it. Our families and close friends may not understand what we are going through because it is not their particular test to endure. Some may attempt to analyze our situation to try to figure out why we are going through what we're going through. We may even be judged or misunderstood because of what is taking place in our lives.

But valleys are God's business. He chooses to deal with us in low places to get our attention and cause us to intentionally draw closer to Him.

Valleys can leave us feeling confused, overwhelmed, and frustrated simply because we don't understand the journey we're on. But in the midst of it all, God graciously helps us gain insight and understanding.

Valleys Are Purposeful

Every valley God allows us to walk through has a divine purpose. Passing through one gives us a chance to exercise our faith and cultivate a greater measure of inner strength, preparing us for what God calls us to do. Valleys are strategically designed to draw us closer to

God, and they afford us opportunities to know Him on a deeper level.

Each time we encounter trouble, we are privileged to see and experience another facet of God. No matter how long we've walked with Him, we will never learn all there is to know about God. Seasons of testing also have a unique way of bringing us to a place of introspection and self-discovery, because God unveils the hidden person of the heart and shows us things of which we are otherwise unaware.

Valleys Are Advantageous

Whenever we find ourselves having to endure a difficult season, we should embrace the experience as a time of spiritual growth and discovery, determining within our hearts to experience God afresh. If He allows us to face trouble, it is usually an indication that God has something much greater in store. With a simple shift in perspective, the difficulties we face can help to transform us into the person we were created to be and catapult us into our destiny.

The greatest advantage of walking through a valley is the process of drawing close to God by being desperate for His presence and hearing His voice. Even when He seems distant, God desires to make Himself known to us in the low places in life. He is the same God on the mountaintops as He is in the valleys. At our lowest points, God whispers, "Call to Me, and I will answer you, and show you great and mighty things, which you do not know" (Jeremiah 33:3 NKJV).

Stop for a moment and consider the current season you are in. Whether you are on a mountaintop and things are going quite well, or you are in a low place trying to figure out how to make it through, the question to consider is this: Are you walking closely with the Lord? Do you sense His presence in your life, or does He seem distant or far away?

- **Point to ponder: There is much to be gained by walking through life's valleys.**

Let's pray and ask God to make Himself known to us today:

> *Father*, You said if I called out to You, You would answer and show me great and mighty things I do not know. Please reveal Yourself to me in a special way. Show me the hidden things that need to be revealed. Teach me what I need to know. I am desperate for Your presence. I need to hear Your voice. I cannot make it on my own. In Jesus's name I pray. Amen!

Chapter 3

MY FIRST VALLEY

I was eighteen years old when I passed through my first valley. It was two weeks after my high school graduation, and I was ready to embark upon a new life marked by freedom and independence. It was a time in my life that should have been filled with happiness and excitement, but for me it was just the opposite. I had lost the only man who truly loved me. My precious daddy had gone home to be with the Lord.

I can't adequately express the depth of sorrow that flooded my heart and soul on the night my dad passed away. I was confused about my future and felt lost and hopeless. I knew God was with me, but I wondered what would become of the rest of my life. I was truly at a crossroad and didn't want to go on.

My dad and I were as close as any father and daughter could be. Dad had a heart for God. He was a deacon in the church, and I loved to hear him pray. When I was about seven or eight years old, he gave me my very first Bible for Christmas. I still have that small white leather Bible today.

I cherish the times Dad and I sat at the kitchen table to read the Bible together. During the final months of his life, we had many intimate conversations. Dad shared his heart with me, knowing he wouldn't be with us much longer. It was a sorrowful time, but I was there to listen whenever he needed someone to talk to.

Dad was too sick to make it to my debutante ball or to watch me walk across the stage at my high school graduation, but I knew in my heart he was happy to know that his youngest child was able to graduate from high school. I inherited many good qualities from my dad, like my personality and love for all people, and I also credit him for my entrepreneurial spirit. Before Dad passed away, he realized his dream of owning his own restaurant.

To this day, I miss him more than words can express. I wish he had lived long enough to know my husband, my children, and his great-grandchildren. They sure would have loved and enjoyed one other.

A few days after Dad's passing, one of his friends, seeing that I was overcome with grief, told me how very proud Dad was of me. The last thing I wanted was to disappoint my daddy by not making anything of myself, so hearing those words lit a small flame in my spirit and gave me enough strength and determination to press on.

The days that followed were lonely and filled with tears, especially when the holiday season approached with its memories of Dad coming home loaded down with gifts and special treats from his co-workers, and the aroma of the roasting turkey as I watched Dad baste it. Thanksgiving and Christmas wouldn't be the same without Dad, but God was with me and my family in our season of sorrow.

Losing someone we love is one of the most difficult things we can ever face in life. No one wants to experience grief and sorrow. It's a time when our heart aches for the one we love and had to let go. Our mind is flooded with memories of days gone by and reflections on how life used to be. Loss is painful to bear. Grief seems to come in waves, hitting us without warning while sending our emotions into a downward spiral. At times, sorrow can leave us feeling as if we want to give up on life, on our future, and maybe even on God Himself. But in Christ, giving up is not an option.

Despite how bad it hurts, there is life after loss. We must go on, remembering God is greater than death.

> O death, where is your victory? O death, where is your sting?" . . . But thank God! He gives us victory over sin and death through our Lord Jesus Christ. ~1 Corinthians 15:55, 57

Whether you've lost someone you love through death or divorce, or you've somehow lost your sense of livelihood, suffering loss sends you through a deep valley. The grieving process is not something we can rush. It takes time to heal and feel strong again. But God is faithful. As we turn to Him for comfort, He always heals our hearts and binds our wounds. Jesus said, "God blesses those who mourn, for they will be comforted" (Matthew 5:4).

The loss of my dad was an extremely hard thing to bear at such an early age and significant time in my life, and I had no idea brighter days awaited me on the road ahead. God had good things in store for me. I just didn't know it. Life would become sweet again. In the meantime, however, I was on a course to destiny, unaware.

After losing my dad, I gained the great blessing of coming to know God as Abba Father and cultivating a genuine Father-daughter relationship with Him. I learned to talk with Him just like I had talked with my earthly father. But I didn't realize the value of my relationship with God until I encountered others who lacked this depth of intimacy with the Lord.

It saddens my heart when someone tells me that they can't relate to God as Father because they never had an earthly father or because their relationship with the father they had was not a good one. It's important to know God as Father because it's hard to have heart-to-heart conversations with a Father we don't know.

Whether you have a good relationship with your earthly father or not, whether he is alive on earth or has passed on, you still need to know God as Father, and He desires to reveal His nature as Father to you, His child.

God is known as a "father to the fatherless" (Psalm 68:5), and we actually receive God's very own Spirit when He adopts us as His own children. As His children, we call Him, "Abba, Father" (Romans 8:15), "For his Spirit joins with our spirit to affirm that we are God's children" (Romans 8:16). "See how very much our Father loves us, for he calls us his children, and that is what we are!" (I John 3:1). Our Father loves us with an everlasting, unconditional love.

Having a revelation of God as our Father changes the trajectory of how we cultivate a lifestyle of closeness with Him. There is nothing like being able to run into our Father's loving arms—to jump upon His lap and be nurtured by Him, healed and comforted by His loving hand when life is too much to bear. Knowing God as Father makes all the difference in how we respond to life's valleys and allows us to emerge victorious.

If you have been wounded or abused by your birth father, you may struggle to intimately connect with God. But that never changes the way He feels about you. If this has been your experience, now is a good time to turn it around. All it takes is one heart-to-heart conversation with Father God, who loves you more than you could imagine. When life disappoints you and doesn't go the way you planned, open your heart and give Him room to work in your life.

- **Point to ponder: There is life after loss. God is greater than death.**

Let's pray for God's healing touch in your life:

Heavenly Father, I come to You with a humble heart. I need You to heal me from the effects of loss and the wounds of my past. Please fill my heart with Your peace and love. I invite You in to do what is necessary to help me move forward. In Jesus's name I pray. Amen.

Chapter 4

CLINGING TO GOD

I f there is one thing life has taught me, it's how to cling to God. I'm not ashamed to admit I've become that clingy, needy child who stays right up under her Father's coattail.

I'm referring to Abba Father, of course. He has been with me throughout my life, whether I was grieving a loss or enjoying happy times. Sometimes I tell God, *Lord, You're stuck with me. I'm Yours and You are mine.* It's true. Whether I am staying close to Him or have distanced myself by getting caught up with the things of this world, God never leaves me alone.

When things are going well, we often feel strong and confident, but this can also cause us to become lazy about our relationship with God. During good times, there is no sense of urgency. We may not feel the need to spend quality time in prayer each day, and having daily conversations with Him is just not our top priority.

But a crisis situation has a way of making us keenly aware of our need for God.

Now, from the moment I find myself entering a valley, I begin to dig deeper spiritually. I spend more time seeking God's face rather than His hand. I make sure I listen much more than I speak. I need to hear from God and gain insight about my situation, so I enter into His presence daily, aiming to know the will of the Lord for my life, and experience peace that surpasses my understanding.

Difficult seasons teach us that it's more important to press in closer—to know God and to listen for His voice—than to ask for things that lack eternal value.

The more difficult the situation, the more we must rely on God for help. I often pray, *God, I'm clinging to You with all my might.* I envision myself holding tightly to the hem of His garment and refusing to let go, much like the woman with the issue of blood did when she saw Jesus passing by. "For she thought, 'If I can just touch his robe, I will be healed'" (Matthew 9:21). Or like Jacob, when he wrestled with the angel of the Lord. Jacob wrestled until his hip was out of joint (Genesis 32:25 NKJV). He refused to let go until he received a blessing. Both the woman with the flow of blood and Jacob were desperate and determined to get what they needed from the Lord.

The more effort we put into seeking God's face— His presence—the more diligent we become about the practice. This daily pursuit makes His presence more real and reminds us that He is always with us.

There are times when I may be doing something as simple as washing dishes at my kitchen sink and pause for a moment to think about God. I immediately sense His presence in a tangible way. This is how close He is to those who continue to draw near to Him.

Many years ago, someone told me, "The proof of the passion is in the pursuit." In other words, the sign of whether or not we are truly passionate about our relationship with God is reflected in our pursuit of Him. I believe there are times in our lives when God purposefully hides Himself from us, allowing us to feel that He is distant so we will seek Him more. Especially when we're in a valley.

> The Lord is near to all who call upon Him,
> To all who call upon Him in truth. He will
> fulfill the desire of those who fear Him; He
> will also hear their cry and save them.
> ~Psalm 145:18–19 NKJV

God is a good and loving Father. If we come close to Him, He will come closer to us. We cannot allow anything or anyone to keep us from His presence. Not our busy schedules or feelings of guilt or condemnation over something we've done. Not laziness or the lack of desire. Regardless or our excuses, we must cling to Him with all our might. We must press beyond the distractions that bombard us each day and hinder us from being close to God. If we search for Him with all our hearts, we will surely find Him.

Whether we're in good times or bad, intimacy with God is the key to both surviving and thriving in life. It gets us to the place we are destined to reach.

We find God's great love, peace, comfort, safety, and security in His presence. At the throne of grace, we learn to release our worries and anxieties and allow Him to carry us through any season we find ourselves in.

Even when it feels like He is far away, or that He's not speaking to you, there is something powerful about being diligent and determined. Keep pursuing Him. Refuse to let Him go. You never know when you are only one prayer away from your greatest encounter with God.

But you will never experience that breakthrough if you give up on the journey. Are you passionately pursuing God with all your heart?

- **Point to ponder: Valley experiences cause us to cling to God.**

Let's take a moment to pray:

> *Lord*, I'm desperate for You. I need Your presence in my life now more than ever. I'm determined to prove my love for You by pursuing You with diligence and passion. I'm determined to seek Your face, not just Your hand. I make a fresh commitment to spend time with You first before anything else. In Jesus's name I pray. Amen.

Chapter 5

PLANS, PURPOSES, AND TIMING

When I look back over my life, I realize that nothing happened according to my plans or in my timing. God moves us along the journey as He sees fit. He knows when we need to be stretched, grow, and be better equipped to fulfill His plans and purpose for our lives.

When I was a teenager, I thought I had life all figured out. I told myself I wouldn't get married until I was twenty-six years old.

But God had other plans.

Two years after my dad passed away, I met my husband. I was in college at the time and had no plans for marriage. But from the moment I met him, I knew there was something special about Cliff. He was different from every man I had ever dated, and it wasn't long before I began to develop deep feelings I couldn't explain. I loved him. I didn't really know why. It was . . . supernatural. Cliff eventually proposed, and we got married.

I was only twenty-two years old and busy building a career I enjoyed. Having children early in the marriage sure wasn't part of my plan. But God had me on a course to destiny. At twenty-three, I gave birth to our first child and my plans of building a successful business took a back seat to motherhood. Eventually, I became a stay-at-home mom. My dreams faded fast, and there wasn't much I could do about it. It was as if I had no control over what was happening in my life.

During the early years of my marriage—the first thirteen, to be exact—I walked through another valley, and it was the longest and most challenging valley I'd endured to date. I was young and naive and full of unrealistic expectations. Much of my struggle was the result of spiritual warfare concerning our future and the work to which God called me.

After coming into the awarness that all life was gone, I cried out to God, *My marriage is dead.*

In that moment, the Lord spoke to my heart: *Without a death, there can be no resurrection.*

Those life-changing words filled me with hope. Within three years, God miraculously restored what had appeared to be beyond hope.

When life takes a turn that differs from what we had in mind, it sets us up for disappointment. We are faced with a choice: Will we take an adventure of faith as we put our trust in the Lord and humbly accept His plan for our lives, or will we live a life of frustration and disappointment because we are determined to do things our way? We can continue to make our own plans and wait to see how far we go before we hit a brick wall, or we can seek the Lord and yield to His divine plan for our lives.

Maybe you see a similar pattern when you look back over your life. You may have had dreams of doing something specific with your life, but God had other plans for you. This is when you must take a good look at *yourself* and *your plans* and decide how you will respond.

The Bible tells us, "You can make many plans, but the Lord's purpose will prevail" (Proverbs 19:21).

I experienced many seasons of frustration and disappointment before I finally came to the realization of this one thing:

God has a master plan, and we fit into it.

It's not about us and it never has been. We are a part of God's big picture. It's all about what God wants to accomplish and how and when He wants to accomplish it. Each of us has our place where we fit in and a particular assignment we must fulfill. It may not seem like it right now, but you and I are exactly where God wants us to be in this season. Our job is to discern the times and seasons we're in and embrace them as significant parts of our journey.

It took years for me to accept the timing of my marriage and the births of my children as part of God's master plan. Even fulfilling my call to become an author and teacher did not come in the order I expected.

First, I received the call to preach and teach. A few years later, I discovered a desire to write books. I'd thought it would be the other way around, but the book came first, and then God began to open doors for speaking engagements. God knows what He's doing and the order by which His plans must unfold. He moves not according to our plan or timing, but His.

To experience the resurrection God promised me, I not only had to grow up spiritually, but I also had to develop as a wife and mom, and most of all as a child of God. My thirteen-year valley represented the death of a dream and the healing of a broken heart. The process involved someone else's will as well. God had to work on me and my husband at the same time. I thought I was entering into marital bliss, but instead God enrolled me in spiritual boot camp, shaping and molding me for ministry. I learned how to advance in ranks and earned my status as a prayer general by exercising spiritual strategies on the front lines of battle.

After our daughter grew up, graduated from college, and got married, the news came that I was going to be a grandmother. I still wasn't ready. I was much too young, I thought. In my mind grandmothers were old and gray. How in the world had I arrived at this point? But I had to accept my grandmother status as the blessing it truly was.

Now, seven years later, I have a whole new perspective. I could never imagine life without my little Grace Michelle. She has brought an abundance of joy and laughter into our world. It's like having our daughter all over again. The two of them are so much alike— even their personalities and mannerisms are the same. Now I know the truth. It is a blessing and an honor to be a grandmother. It is an earned status that tells a woman she has arrived at a place of wisdom and honor.

Father really does know best. Value and ease come from trusting His plan in every season of life. Gaining the right point of view about God's timing takes away the frustration and responsibility of trying to make things happen when we think they should.

When we hit a low place in life, we often wonder how long the season will last or why a certain thing we've been praying for and waiting on hasn't happened yet. We must realize that these matters belong to God. He sets the times and seasons of our lives and has predetermined when we will step into our destiny. He alone can bring it to pass.

Although uncomfortable and full of uncertainty and unanswered questions, life's valleys help us turn our attention toward God and rest in His abiding love for us. We must trust that He will not leave us in a place of transition beyond our ability to endure it. God takes no pleasure in watching His children suffer. Every valley God allows us to pass through has a divine purpose. And it's always greater than any pain and suffering we have to endure.

I look back in amazement at all the Lord has accomplished in my life and family since I entered that valley. For me and Cliff, marriage is sweeter today than we ever thought possible, and we are convinced it will grow sweeter still. We laugh together, travel together, go on date nights and to sporting events, and have lots of fun as a couple. Yes, we face trials together, but we get through them. God has blessed our union to be very fruitful, and we are forever thankful!

The Bible tells us, "But I trusted in, relied on, and was confident in You, O Lord; I said, You are my God.

My times are in Your hands" (Psalm 31:14–15 AMPC). We must yield to God's plan and His timing for our lives. Anything short of that will only bring frustration and disappointment.

- **Point to ponder: For every valley God allows us to pass through, He has a divine plan and purpose.**

Let's pray:

> *Lord God*, help me to trust in Your timing. You know what is best for me. I realize You have a master plan, and I simply fit into it. Thank You or allowing me to be a part of Your big picture for mankind and for Your Kingdom. I yield to Your plan, purpose, and timing in my life. In Jesus's name I pray. Amen.

Chapter 6

GOD HAS A GOOD PLAN

It's difficult to grasp the concept of how suffering can be part of God's *good* plan for our lives, so we must focus on what awaits us on the other side. God does not enjoy watching us suffer, but He observes how we process our pain and suffering as we wait for the glorious outcome. If we walk by faith instead of according to our senses, we will come out with the blessing and reward that God intended for us from the very beginning.

God sent His only begotten Son to die on a cross so we could have life everlasting. He considered us worth it. God knew He would gain many more children because of the sacrifice of one. We may not have a clear view of the outcome of our suffering while we are going through it, but if we endure the test we will see how God uses it in our lives for good. He also has a way of making it up to us. Our purpose—or better yet, God's purpose for our lives—is always greater than our pain. Suffering is selfless. It causes us to move our gaze from ourselves and our personal desires and focus instead on the Lord.

No matter how hard it is or how bad it hurts, if we hold on to the hope that we have in Christ, we can make it through anything. Endurance is an expression of our faith and trust in Him. Come what may, we must trust that God's master plan is always a good one. Our willingness to trust and total surrender to God's plan is what pleases Him most.

From firsthand experience, Jesus understands what it's like to endure the pain of rejection, sorrow, shame, and even fear. When He was on earth, He stood firm in the face of opposition by refusing to give up or give in. As we look to Jesus, the Author and Finisher of our faith, it helps us to withstand our valley experiences and stand strong.

Jesus spent thirty-three years on earth as a natural man. If we pause to consider His suffering and ultimate sacrifice, it's hard to justify being weary or giving up when we are in a low place. In life's valleys we must remember Jesus, knowing God has a good plan and a higher purpose in mind. We will endure as Jesus did, and we will fulfill God's plan for our lives and accomplish what we are here on earth to accomplish.

> He was despised and rejected—a man of sorrows, acquainted with deepest grief. We turned our backs on him and looked the other way. He was despised, and we did not care. . . . But it was the LORD's good plan to crush him and cause him grief. Yet when his life is made an offering for sin, he will have many descendants. ~Isaiah 53:3, 10

Jesus suffered to make a way for us to become children of God. Now that we are God's children, we must also fellowship in the Lord's sufferings. When God seems silent, we must practice what we know, relying on the Word of God and resting in what He has already spoken.

If you have ever taken a test in school, you may remember this principle: the teacher is always silent during the test. Knowing they've already taught the material, when test day comes, the teacher expects the students to apply that knowledge accordingly. Likewise, during times of trouble and distress, those of us who have already been taught must dig deep, rely on what we already know about our God, and stand on His Word. We must then apply that knowledge to our circumstances.

The Earth Was His Valley

If anyone deserved the royal treatment from birth it was Jesus. And yet, as the only begotten Son of the Father, He humbled Himself and became a servant, obedient even to the point of death on a cross. Jesus left the beauty and splendor of heaven to come *down* to earth. He was brought low so that we could go high and receive eternal life.

[But He ascended?] Now what can this, He ascended, mean but that He had previously descended from [the heights of] heaven into [the depths], the lower parts of the earth? He Who descended is the [very] same as He Who

> also has ascended high above all the heavens,
> that He [His presence] might fill all things
> (the whole universe, from the lowest to the
> highest). ~Ephesians 4:9–10 AMPC

Jesus truly humbled Himself so we could receive what we need during our lives on earth and throughout eternity. If we consider what life must have been like for Jesus while He was on earth, we will clearly see that things were not easy or perfect for our Savior. But He was on a mission to fulfill God's good plan.

Although He was Emmanuel—God with us—Jesus had a meek and humble beginning. He was born in a manger among animals because there was no room for Him in the inn. As if that wasn't enough, His parents were forced to move from place to place to keep Him safe from harm. Threatened by the fulfillment of a prophecy (that the Christ Child, the Messiah had been born), King Herod had ordered all the male children two years of age and younger to be murdered. You'd think God would have arranged for things to be perfect for our beloved Savior and His family, but they were not. How could it be that God's own Son had to endure such a life of suffering in order to fulfill His purpose? If Jesus was allowed to suffer, why should our lives on earth be exempt from suffering?

> Even though Jesus was God's Son, he learned obedience from the things he suffered. In this way, God qualified him as a perfect High Priest, and he became the source of

eternal salvation for all those who obey him.
~Hebrews 5:8, 9

It may not seem fair or make sense to us, but when we consider that Jesus suffered unjustly, we know we are in good company. Jesus's life was not an easy one, yet for the joy that was set before Him, He endured. He went about doing good, healing the sick, raising the dead, and casting out demons as people cried out to Him for help. I'm sure there were times when Jesus felt overwhelmed by the needs of humanity and the constant pull of people. It's the same for many of us today.

The needs around us are great and many. People demand our time and attention. But we must follow the example Jesus set for us. Time and again, He showed us how to handle life's pressures. He often withdrew from the crowd and His closest followers to find a quiet place to pray. This intimate time alone with the Father prepared Him for his most difficult test of all. The cross.

Staying Focused

As Jesus faced death, all He could do was look to God and focus on the glory that would be revealed. His total dependence and reliance was on his Father. This season of suffering and death did not represent a place of finality. Rather it was a passageway from this earthly valley—where He spent thirty-three years having a human experience—back to His heavenly home and His position of glory and honor, seated at the right hand of the Father.

In Psalm 16, David penned a prophetic prayer, beautifully conveying Jesus's heart as He endured suffering and death on the cross. It shows us the importance of fixing our gaze on God as He works His master plan in our lives and brings it into fulfillment. As we walk with Him through tough places, God will not leave us alone. Neither will He allow us to stay where we are at the present time. We can trust in God's love, mercy, and ultimate plan for our lives as we come to a place of total surrender and complete rest, knowing that our future is in God's hands. We can be assured that God's plan is a good one. Despite what we encounter on our journeys, we can count on Him to usher us into our destiny.

Prophetic Prayers to Encourage you

> I know the LORD is always with me. I will not be shaken, for he is right beside me. No wonder my heart is glad, and I rejoice. My body rests in safety. For you will not leave my soul among the dead or allow your holy one to rot in the grave. You will show me the way of life, granting me the joy of your presence and the pleasures of living with you forever.
> ~Psalm 16:8–11

> I love the LORD, because He has heard [and now hears] my voice and my supplications. Because He has inclined His ear to me, therefore will I call upon Him as long as I live. . . . Then called I upon the name of the Lord: O Lord, I beseech You, save my life *and* deliver me! Gracious is the LORD, and

[rigidly] righteous; yes, our God is merciful. The Lord preserves the simple; I was brought low, and He helped *and* saved me. Return to your rest, O my soul, for the Lord has dealt bountifully with you. For You have delivered my life from death, my eyes from tears, and my feet from stumbling *and* falling. I will walk before the Lord in the land of the living. I believed (trusted in, relied on, and clung to my God), and therefore have I spoken [even when I said], I am greatly afflicted. ~Psalm 116:1–2, 4–10 AMPC

You may not understand God's plan for your life, but like Jesus, you must look ahead to see the glory that awaits you on the other side of every valley you are allowed to walk through.

- **Point to ponder: God's plan requires complete trust.**

Let's pray a prayer of surrender as we place our total trust in God and His faithfulness:

Father God, help me to accept Your good plan for my life. Even when things don't turn out the way I expect them to, and when I am faced with difficulty, I will trust in You. I know You want the very best for my life. Please give me the strength to endure this season of suffering, so that You may be glorified through it all. In Jesus's name I pray. Amen.

Chapter 7

PREPARING FOR PURPOSE

There are times when the sovereign will of God leads us to places we would rather not go. It seems unfair and even impossible when we obey God, seek to please Him, and follow His will for our lives, and still end up in a valley. But it happens, and it prepares us for our future.

After Jesus was baptized by John, the Holy Spirit descended in bodily form like a dove upon Him, and a voice came from heaven which said, "You are My beloved Son; in You I am well pleased" (Luke 3:22 NKJV). Right after His glorious experience, however, the Bible reports, "Then Jesus, being filled with the Holy Spirit, returned from the Jordan and was led by the Spirit into the wilderness" (Luke 4:1 NKJV).

Looking at the way the events of Jesus's life unfolded as He fulfilled His earthly purpose, we can see a similar pattern in our lives as children of God.

His story continues to enlighten ours. During a season of fasting and prayer Jesus had not eaten for forty days and nights. Afterward He was hungry (v. 2). When He was at His weakest point, Satan tried to tempt and test Jesus, hoping He would question His true identity. But Jesus knew who He was even when many did not believe Him.

Jesus is our ultimate example of what it means to walk in our true identity. From Him we learn how we are to respond when the Enemy casts doubt on who we are in Christ.

I believe Satan wondered if Jesus was the true Messiah, the Son of the living God. He said, "*If* you are the Son of God, tell this stone to become a loaf of bread" (v. 3). But Jesus stood firm and refused to allow the devil to steal His confidence, answering, "No! The Scriptures say, 'People do not live by bread alone'" (v. 4).

After failing at his first attempt, the devil took Jesus to a high place and showed Him all the kingdoms of the world in a moment's time. Jesus was taken from a low place in the wilderness to a high one and promised all the authority over the earth and the glory that went with it. All Jesus had to do was bow down and worship the devil.

This is so typical of the Enemy. He likes to dangle carrots in front of us to lure us away from God's plan for our lives, and into a counterfeit plan.

Once again, however, Jesus responded with Scripture. "You must worship the LORD your God and serve only him" (v. 8).

After two failed attempts, the devil took Jesus to Jerusalem, to the pinnacle of the temple, trying to convince Him to throw Himself off and basically commit suicide, thereby thwarting God's purpose. Satan went as far as to quote Scripture by telling Jesus that the angels would hold Him up and keep Him from hurting His foot on a stone (vv. 10–11).

Again, Jesus fought back with the Word: "The Scriptures also say, 'You must not test the LORD your God'" (v. 12). Satan then left Him.

When Satan comes to tempt us to doubt who we are in Christ and to hinder us from fulfilling our purpose as children of God, we must always answer the adversary with the Word of God.

Satan was bold enough to try to tempt Jesus, the Son of God. In our moments of human weakness, he will not hesitate to cast a cloud of doubt over our minds concerning who we are and what we are called to do. This is a common occurrence. When we're in a valley, surrounded by questions and uncertainty, weak and tired from the battle, our identity will be put to the test.

Our adversary would love to convince us to exchange the struggles and suffering of the Christian life for whatever the world has to offer. But this is no fair exchange. The kingdom of God is far greater than the kingdoms of this world.

Fight Back with the Word of God

We can glean many lessons and insights from Jesus's wilderness experience. The most important lesson of all is learning to fight every temptation by speaking God's Word aloud.

If we expect to overcome and be successful in our most difficult seasons of life, we must know what God's Word has to say about who we are in Christ. We must fill up on Scripture during the good times so we can pull from the reservoir deep within our hearts when times are hard. God promises to combat every lie of the Enemy. Hidden in our hearts, the Word will rise to the surface when we need it most. If we ever come to know who we really are in Christ, no demon from hell can stop us from moving into our destiny and fulfilling our God-given purpose.

As we walk through life's valleys as Jesus did, we will come out with an awareness of our spiritual authority. We will recognize the power of God that is resident within us through the person of the Holy Spirit. He is the same Spirit who raised Jesus from the dead, and He lives in us. Isn't that amazing? Every time we endure a test or trial and come out on the other side, we gain a degree of boldness and courage we didn't possess before. This is how we grow up spiritually and learn to walk in the assurance of our true identity in Christ.

> Then Jesus returned in the power of the Spirit to Galilee, and news of Him went out through all the surrounding region.
> ~v. 14 NKJV

The Enemy failed in his attempt to make Jesus doubt His identity and abort His mission to redeem mankind. Instead, God used this testing to fortify Jesus and prepare Him for purpose.

Jesus fasted and prayed for forty days and nights, seeking the Father and positioning Himself for service. Although He felt weak in body, He was strong in spirit. This is how we, too, are guaranteed victory over the Enemy. It can offer us encouragement and joy as we walk through difficult places.

Every test and trial we endure has the potential to yield a greater glory if we stand firm in our faith and know our true identity as blood-bought children of the Most High God. If we are convinced of who we are in Christ and what we are called to do, no enemy can stop us!

After the Test

After Jesus's season of testing ended, He went forth and did what God sent Him to do. He began to fulfill His purpose on earth. The Word tells us that Jesus taught regularly in their synagogues and was praised by everyone (v. 15). I am not implying that we should seek the praise and glory of man. When we come out on the other side of our test having gained the victory, God is glorified through the word of our testimony. If we gain a kingdom perspective of our situation and refuse to faint, give up, or give into the devil's temptations, we will be catapulted into higher realms of glory as we fulfill our purpose.

> And after you have suffered a little while, the God of all grace [Who imparts all blessing and favor], Who has called you to His [own] eternal glory in Christ *Jesus*, will Himself

complete *and* make you what you ought to be, establish *and* ground you securely, and strengthen, and settle you. ~1 Peter 5:10 AMPC

Each of us has a kingdom assignment to accomplish. You—yes, you—have something special and unique to do for God. Valleys are designed to help prepare and strengthen you to fulfill your purpose.

- **Point to ponder: Valleys prepare and strengthen us to fulfill our God-given purpose.**

Let's pray a prayer of thanksgiving as we prepare to move into our God-given destiny:

Father, thank You for keeping me in Your care and protection. For never leaving me or forsaking me, especially in my season of testing. And for establishing me and strengthening and making me who You destined me to become. Thank You for preparing me for the work You have called me to. I know I can do all things through Christ who gives me strength. In Jesus's name I pray. Amen.

Chapter 8

IT COMES WITH THE TERRITORY

One of my favorite things to do as a kid was pretending to be a nurse. With clipboard in hand, I called my imaginary patients from the waiting room (my parents' living room) to come in to see the doctor. I played this for hours, allowing my imagination to run wild. It gave me a sense of great joy and fulfillment to help people, even when I was just pretending.

I never became a nurse, mainly due to my dislike of chemistry, which was one of the most difficult subjects for me in school. But God had other plans for my life. Considering the work that I'm doing today as an author, speaker, and teacher, the compassion He placed in my heart for people makes a lot of sense.

God called me to preach and teach His Word specifically in the area of prayer and intercession a few years after I became a wife and mom. The call to ministry changed the entire trajectory of my life and sent me on a course to destiny. I've endured many seasons of testing to arrive at where I am today. During those seasons, I didn't understand what God was doing or why He would allow me to go through those difficulties. But as

I look back now, I see how each valley I passed through was a part of the preparation process.

I believe that most kindhearted and compassionate people want to make a difference in the world. They have a desire to know their life's purpose and be about the business of fulfilling it. When we start out on our journey toward the fulfillment of our calling, however, we are unaware of the price we will have to pay for it and what we will encounter along the way. But God never wastes suffering and hardship. Instead, He uses them to prepare us for our purpose.

We must be willing to go through a preparation process in order to do what God has called us to do. Even if we are born with a natural inclination or gifting in a certain area—like my love and compassion for people and heart to help others—none of us are fully prepared to fulfill our assignment at the start. We need time and experience to help us mature.

I needed to be taught the Word of God and trained through life experiences. I had to learn how to stand strong in the Lord, wage war against the attacks of the Enemy, and be victorious.

There are things that must be imparted to us so we can be effective in the particular area we are called to impact. Other things must be removed or taken away. God has a way of using our circumstances to rid us of the things that cannot go with us into our future. For example, we may need to bid farewell to certain attitudes and mindsets that produce pride, fear, a low view of ourselves, feelings of rejection, and so much more.

These things have no place in our lives if we want to be used by God.

We must learn to endure the trials that test our faith and strengthen our character, so that we're able to handle what lies ahead.

Certain challenges are to be expected within our holy assignments. When he was a shepherd boy tending his father's flock, David learned to conquer a bear and a lion. That fight prepared him to defeat Goliath, the Philistine giant who prided himself in defying the armies of the Lord. Defeating Goliath prepared David for his future reign as a conquering king. Let's ignite our faith by taking a look at a few highlights from David's story in I Samuel 17.

> Saul countered by gathering his Israelite troops near the valley of Elah. So the Philistines and Israelites faced each other on opposite hills, with the valley between them. Then Goliath, a Philistine champion from Gath, came out of the Philistine ranks to face the forces of Israel. He was over nine feet tall. Goliath stood and shouted a taunt across to the Israelites. . . . "Why are you all coming out to fight?" he called. "I am the Philistine champion, but you are only the servants of Saul. Choose one man to come down here and fight me!" (vv. 2–4, 8)

> But David persisted. "I have been taking care of my father's sheep and goats," he said.

"When a lion or a bear comes to steal a lamb from the flock, I go after it with a club and rescue the lamb from its mouth. If the animal turns on me, I catch it by the jaw and club it to death. I have done this to both lions and bears, and I'll do it to this pagan Philistine, too, for he has defied the armies of the living God!" (vv. 34–36). So David triumphed over the Philistine with only a sling and a stone, for he had no sword. Then David ran over and pulled Goliath's sword from its sheath. David used it to kill him and cut off his head. (vv. 50–51).

It's interesting that David had to go down into a valley to face the battle that set him on course to destiny, but as a result of his victory, he received a promotion and many rewards. Like David, we must never despise our season of training and preparation, despite how long it lasts. Instead, we should thank God for loving us enough to use our circumstances to thoroughly train and prepare us for the next level. He is getting us ready for our future, preparing us to conquer in the arena to which we are called, and providing us with the ability to slay any giant that comes to hinder our progress toward receiving God's promises.

Today, despite what comes against us, let's see ourselves as more than conquerors in Christ.

Are you in a season of preparation? Are you surprised by the level of attack against you? What are some of the ways God is preparing you for your future?

- **Point to ponder: Valleys help to develop our character and equip us to handle what lies ahead.**

Let's take a moment to pray:

Father God, I may not understand why You are allowing me to face such difficulty in my life, but I trust that You are preparing me for the future and the work You have called me to. Help me to stand strong on Your promises. I want to pass this test and walk in victory over my enemies. In Jesus's name I pray. Amen!

Chapter 9

SHARING IN CHRIST'S SUFFERING

When I was young, I didn't give much thought to my health and eating habits. I was skinny and could eat whatever I wanted. But over the years I've come to understand the importance of exercising, eating right, and staying on top of my health. It's now a priority.

My husband and I get yearly physicals and screenings to make sure we are in optimal health. After a routine colonoscopy and endoscopy, I returned home and felt a lump in my throat whenever I swallowed. When I visited my primary care physician to investigate the problem, he referred me to an endocrinologist.

After introducing himself and asking me a few questions, the endocrinologist lowered the lights to take a closer look at my thyroid via sonogram. When he turned the lights back up, the look on his face could have filled my heart with terror.

"Ma'am, you have a mass on the right side of your thyroid," he said. "It is a very large mass, and it may be cancerous. But we won't know until we remove it."

After the initial shock, tears filled my eyes. My heart raced. When I composed myself, I headed for home, resisting the spirit of fear that tried to grip me.

When I arrived home, I went into my office, sat at my desk, and quieted myself before the Lord. It wasn't long before I asked the big question: *Lord, am I going to have to have surgery, or are You going to supernaturally heal me?*

I knew God could do anything. I had witnessed His miraculous healing power many times before. He had healed me of scoliosis and migraine headaches in the early years of my marriage. I knew He could heal me with one simple touch.

It wasn't long before God spoke to my heart with tenderness and compassion. But He spoke words I didn't want to hear.

I will allow you to be cut on, but I will be glorified.

I had a sense of peace and the assurance that, even though I had to go through surgery, everything would turn out fine. God was going to get the glory for my story, and that was all that mattered to me.

I had no idea that a long and difficult journey lay ahead.

God, in His mercy, gives us clues and indications to let us know when we are about to enter a valley or a season of testing.

> And since we are his children, we are his heirs.
> In fact, together with Christ we are heirs of
> God's glory. But if we are to share his glory,
> we must also share his suffering. Yet what we

suffer now is nothing compared to the glory
he will reveal to us later.   ~Romans 8:17–18

It's hard to describe the feelings that flood our hearts and the thoughts that fill our minds when we realize we are entering a valley. There is a great deal of uncertainty about what we will have to endure and how long the season will last. But valley experiences are inevitable and a normal part of life. Whether we are good or bad, obedient or disobedient, male or female, Christian or unbeliever, and regardless of race or financial status, everyone walks through valleys. We can't get around them, we must walk through them. Each of us is either entering a valley, walking through one, or coming out on the other side.

Suffering Silently

Some of life's valleys are isolating. When I received my thyroid diagnosis, no one could help me or spare me from this test. My family loved me, but this was something I had to walk through on my own. It was my faith, not someone else's, going on trial. There were days when I felt down and questioned, *Why?* I'd gone through several surgeries in the past, but this one was different. I didn't know if the mass was cancerous or not. I had to trust God. He was all I had to hold on to.

Whether others are watching to see what the outcome will be or you are suffering silently, no one will ever know the depths of your suffering or the level of your brokenness and disappointment like God. That's the way He designed it to be. When you are at your lowest, God wants you to come to Him and allow Him to walk close beside you. He wants to teach you things. He wants to reveal secrets to you. He wants to impart things into your spirit. He wants you to look back on this time in your life and recognize that He was the One who brought you safely through it. Therefore, He alone gets all the glory. No one else.

Trusting God When We Don't Understand

After visiting two different surgeons and going through extensive testing, the day of my surgery finally arrived. When I checked into the hospital and was taken to my room, I felt like an innocent lamb being led to the slaughter. I had no idea what was about to transpire, but I trusted God for the outcome and held tightly to the words He had spoken to my heart months before: *I will allow you to be cut on, but I will be glorified.*

My husband was told that the surgery would last two and a half hours, but it took twice as long. The mass had grown out of control. Four and a half hours later, I opened my eyes in the recovery room feeling like I'd been hit by a truck. When the surgeon came in to check on me, she said my mass was one of the worst cases she had ever seen. When she asked me how I felt and when I tried to answer, I was utterly shocked by the sound of my voice. It sounded like I had a horrible case of laryngitis.

The doctor assured me that my voice should improve within a few months. I didn't know what that meant, but I was glad to be alive and that no cancer was found. God had proven faithful, and I knew He would see me through. I was in the midst of a valley, and there was nothing I could do to change it.

When we are going through a valley, we often become perplexed by what is happening to us, and rightly so. Pride demands to understand what's going on, while trust surrenders the matter to God, placing it in His capable hands. God is the One who determines the depth of our valleys and the length of our journey. He knows the amount of work He needs to accomplish in our lives, even when we think we're doing just fine. But the more we yield to God and surrender our will to His, the faster we complete the process. The more we know and understand of the depths of God's great love and compassion for us, the more we trust and rest in Him. Even when nothing makes sense to us. We must come to the place where we simply accept God's grace as sufficient enough to sustain us in times of trouble.

> LORD, my heart is not proud; my eyes are not haughty. I don't concern myself with matters too great or too awesome for me to grasp. Instead, I have calmed and quieted myself, like a weaned child who no longer cries for its mother's milk. Yes, like a weaned child is my soul within me. ~Psalms 131:1–3

Are you struggling to understand the season you're in? If so, that's to be expected. It's part of our human nature. Your mind and heart may be filled with questions, but God will give insight and understanding concerning the work He's doing in your life at His appointed time. We can ask God for understanding as often as we feel the need, but He speaks when He is ready.

God's silence beckons us to continue to walk with Him and place our trust in Him as we seek His face in prayer. God wants us to fully surrender our situation to Him, patiently waiting until He reveals what we need to know.

God Works While We Rest

As I recovered at home, discouragement began to set in. Christmastime approached, and I had intended to spend the month of December promoting my first book, *Pray-ers Bear Fruit*, which had released in November of the previous year. This was the first holiday season when I could launch a solid marketing campaign to share with others. Unfortunately, I had no voice or strength to execute my plan.

We think our plan is right—or the *only* plan—until God shows up with His *ultimate* plan. When we trust Him and get out of His way, God always takes care of us. The Bible tells us, "The LORD will perfect that which concerns me; Your mercy, O LORD, endures forever; Do not forsake the works of Your hands" (Psalm 138:8 NKJV).

God proved His faithful love to me and taught me a valuable lesson at the same time. While my heart and intentions may have been noble, God let me know that

He didn't need my help. He was more than able to do something far beyond what I could ask or think.

I received a message from a friend who had just received the tragic news that her husband's parents were killed in a car accident. She shared with me that she knew God was with her when she tuned in to a local Christian radio station and heard my voice speaking loud and clear. I was taken aback. How could this be possible when I was lying in bed recovering from surgery? As it turned out, the radio station was airing a previously recorded interview where I discussed the power of prayer along with my book, *Pray-ers Bear Fruit*.

All I could do was cry. While I had no voice or strength to promote my book or its message, God still used my voice to encourage my friend in her season of sorrow, as well as countless others who listened to the show. In His lovingkindness and tenderness, God often reveals Himself when we are feeling low and discouraged.

As children of God, we must fight to stay in faith. The Enemy never fights fair. His MO is to attack us when we're at our weakest point. He tries to leverage every opportunity to tempt us to give up on God and ourselves, because he wants us to thwart God's plan and purpose for our lives. But if we know who we are in Christ and what God has spoken to us, the Enemy will lose every battle. The truth is, we are in a fixed fight and destined to win. We cannot quit or give up on God before He finishes working His plan and teaching us what He wants us to know. When the devil sees our persistence in walking with God come what may, and when he sees he is failing to make progress with us, he eventually gives up and waits for another opportunity.

Are you battling thoughts of discouragement and defeat because things are not working out according to your plan? Know this: whenever our plans fail to work out, it means God has a greater plan in place.

I don't know about you, but I'd much rather follow God's plan than mine. Even if it involves suffering, God's plan always has the best outcome.

- **Point to ponder: If we want to share in God's glory, we must be willing to share in the suffering.**

Let's pray:

> *Father*, I surrender my will to Yours. I release my disappointments and frustrations when things don't go the way I planned. Help me to move out of Your way and allow Your will to be accomplished. Thank You for always having my best interest at heart and for working everything out for my good. In Jesus's name I pray. Amen.

Chapter 10

THE NECESSITY OF HUMILITY

It is a part of our human nature to think we are better off than we really are. We may think our hearts are pure and our motives sincere concerning the things we want out of life. But only God knows the true condition of a person's heart. The truth is often revealed when we are confronted by pressure or life doesn't go our way. When we are squeezed, low, broken, or miserable, what's hidden on the inside will eventually come out of us.

Suffering brings us to our knees. When we're in trouble, most of us approach prayer with a greater fervency and tenacity than when things were going well. Valleys force us to get real with God and cry out to Him from a sincere place. They are designed to cultivate true humility and transparency within us before God. When we are willing to face whatever He chooses to reveal, He will shine His light upon us so we are aware of our flaws and weaknesses. Once we face the cold, hard facts about ourselves, things will begin to change. God exposes the hidden matters of the heart and does business with His children in low places.

I remember the day I heard God speak to my heart, *Meet Me in the valley.* I knew in that moment, during one of the most difficult times in my life, He was beckoning me closer for a specific purpose. God was calling me into a deeper level of intimacy with Him to reveal the rich treasures of the secret place that can only be obtained in times of trouble. I was intrigued by His words. Although being in a valley can have negative connotations, there is something that compels us to enter it with great expectancy for what God is about to do.

When we find ourselves in the midst of a valley, we can cease from worrying, fretting, squirming, and screaming about whatever we deem to be important and get quiet before God. We can allow Him to speak to us afresh. It's always amazing what He reveals. This process often leads to a promotion from the Lord as He lifts us to places of honor that only He can give.

God Corrects Those He Loves

God sometimes uses the most unlikely circumstances as a means to correct and discipline us, because He is a loving Father. Several months after my surgery, I returned to my doctor for a follow-up appointment. After hearing the sound of my voice and seeing that there was very little improvement, I was sent to two different specialists, an ENT (ear, nose, and throat doctor), and a laryngologist (a doctor who specializes in disorders of the larynx and vocal cords) who was considered one of the best in the state of Texas.

The doctor's report wasn't at all what I anticipated. After undergoing several very uncomfortable tests that allowed the doctors to take a close look at my vocal cords, I was diagnosed with vocal cord paralysis. I was shocked by the diagnosis. My right vocal cord—the side where the mass had been located—failed to move when I spoke.

How could God allow this to happen to me? I had trusted Him about moving forward with the surgery. I thought everything was supposed to turn out fine. To say I was disappointed would be an understatement. I was perplexed.

Questions flooded my heart and mind as I sunk into despair. If God had truly called me to preach and teach others how to pray, how could I accomplish my assignment with the little voice that remained?

My vocal ability was unpredictable. People could barely hear me much of the time. Other times my voice sounded raspy and cracked when I spoke. It was a frightening, often embarrassing predicament. When I opened my mouth, I never knew what sound would come out.

Beyond my vocal issues, I also had to learn how to swallow liquids without choking. Even the slightest bit of pepper or anything spicy would settle around my vocal cord and cause me to cough uncontrollably, making it difficult to catch my breath. It was so discouraging that I was tempted to stop using my voice entirely, to withdraw from going out in public, to speak only when absolutely necessary and avoid the discomfort. I felt life would be easier that way.

I tend to be rather quiet and reserved when I meet someone for the first time. I was taught that you only get one chance to make a good first impression; therefore, my image and personal appearance have always been important to me, even as a teenager. I guess it was just the way my mother raised me, but I share this to help you gain a better understanding of the degree of "dying to self" that needed to take place in my life during this season. God knew I cared a little too much about my personal image and what others thought of me, and He was about to do something about it.

> Search me, O God, and know my heart; test me and know my anxious thoughts. Point out anything in me that offends you, and lead me along the path of everlasting life.
> ~Psalm 139:23–24

The days to come were filled with one humbling experience after another.

If I talked to my daughter in line at the grocery story, it wasn't uncommon for someone in front of us to jerk their head around to catch a glimpse of where the weird voice was coming from. At the drive-through windows of fast food restaurants, cashiers would say something like, "Ma'am, I can't hear you. You have to speak up." I got so tired of dealing with it that I eventually started driving past the intercom box and went straight to the window to place my order.

On another occasion, I called to schedule an appointment over the telephone and the woman who answered laughed out loud at the sound of my voice. It really hurt my heart. I wanted to say something, but I held my peace.

At the wedding reception for a friend's son, a woman I'd never met before, clearly under the assumption that the softness of my voice was the result of shyness or timidity, said, "Girl, speak up! Can't nobody hear you!" By that time, I was tired of comments like this, so I spoke up and told the woman I had a paralyzed vocal cord. Needless to say, she felt terrible. I assured her it was okay.

These are just a few of the many experiences that led to a great deal of frustration in my life. I was ashamed of the sound of my own voice. I couldn't hide it anymore. My issues of shame and insecurity had risen to the surface, and questions flooded my mind.

What did I do wrong?

What did I do to deserve this?

Why was God allowing this to happen to me?

Why me?

This season lasted four years, but God was doing a deep work in my life by allowing me to face these daily challenges, stretching me, and growing me up to take me to another level. The journey was long and the road difficult to bear, but in God's presence, it was filled with wonder and delight.

There is so much more I could share about this time in my life, but I think you get the picture. The inner workings of God in my heart had just as much significance as the healing and restoration of my voice.

Through these embarrassing encounters, God exposed heart issues that needed to be addressed before I could move forward with my assignment.

> So humble yourselves under the mighty power of God, and at the right time he will lift you up in honor. ~1 Peter 5:6

As I sought the Lord with questions—sometimes in a tone that I'm now ashamed to admit using—He revealed that I had impure motives in my heart.

Impure motives? Who, me?

I was totally unaware of my need to be transformed on the inside until God exposed my heart. I wanted people to think highly of me. I wanted to sound good. I wanted to make a good impression. I cared about how others perceived me.

Have you noticed how many times I've used the word *I*?

I was focused on myself, but God wanted to teach me that the process wasn't about me. None of the things I was concerned about mattered to God. He wanted to purge me of them. Over that time, I learned four valuable lessons that apply to everyone who desires to be used by God. Maybe they will resonate with you as well:

> Lesson One: God wants everything we do to be for His glory, not ours.

> Lesson Two: God wants us to exercise our faith even in the face of embarrassment and shame.

Lesson Three: God wants us to trust Him even when nothing makes sense.

Lesson Four: God wants our confidence to stem from a place of security in Him, not from having confidence in ourselves.

But you desire honesty from the womb, teaching me wisdom even there. Purify me from my sins, and I will be clean; wash me, and I will be whiter than snow.
~Psalm 51:6–7

We lack understanding as to why God allows us to go through certain tests and trials as we walk through life's valleys. But through suffering He exposes what is hidden within and purges us of everything that needs to be removed, making us fit for His use.

Wherever we find ourselves in a low place, God has an opportunity to unveil the motives and intents of our hearts.

We shouldn't be surprised when God reveals what is hidden within our hearts when we go through hard times. We should gladly welcome His correction because He loves us enough to change us and clean us up. No matter what He exposes, we can consider ourselves blessed, knowing God only corrects those He loves—those who truly belong to Him.

And have you forgotten the encouraging words God spoke to you as his children? He said, "My child, don't make light of the

Lord's discipline, and don't give up when he corrects you. For the Lord disciplines those he loves, and he punishes each one he accepts as his child." As you endure this divine discipline, remember that God is treating you as his own children. Who ever heard of a child who is never disciplined by its father? If God doesn't discipline you as he does all of his children, it means that you are illegitimate and are not really his children at all. ⁓Hebrews 12:5–8.

A valley is the perfect place to search our hearts and ask ourselves if we're there due to disobedience or by God's divine providence. Remember, Jesus did nothing to warrant His wilderness or valley experience. In fact, His baptism was pleasing to the Father. But He was led into a time of testing for a specific purpose.

If we understand why we are in a season of testing, when the tempter comes to accuse us or torment us with fear, doubt, and unbelief, we will have the correct response. We can usually discover the reason for our valley experience by a simple process of elimination.

When we examine our hearts and actions leading up to this time in our lives, we can easily decipher whether we're in a season of correction or of testing. If God is correcting us, we can be encouraged by the words of Hebrews 12:5–8. If we're in a time of testing, we can also be encouraged because God is preparing us for where we're going, and there are lessons to be learned in the process.

Over the years I've noticed that the seasons of my life seem to fall into one of three categories:

1. Seasons of Correction: Because He loves me, God takes me through a process of correction for something I have done wrong. (See Hebrews 12:5–11.)

2. Seasons of Temptation, Test, or Trial: God allows me to be tempted, tested, or tried in order to reveal what's in my heart and to prepare me for my purpose. The devil comes only to steal, kill, and destroy; he attacks my mind, my physical body, my relationships, or my finances. The Enemy is incapable of creating anything new, so he repackages the same old tricks.   (See James 1:1–4, 13–15.)

3. Seasons of Rewards and Blessings: These are the times when I feel the happiest—when God rewards me outwardly for what I've done in secret. During these seasons I enjoy a good harvest based on the goodness of the Lord and the good seeds I have sown. (See Matthew 6:6; Galatians 6:7.)

- **Point to ponder: Being in a valley is humbling. It causes what is hidden in our hearts to come to the surface.**

Let's pray:

> *Father God*, I humbly bow before You. I repent of sins known and unknown, of anything that has been displeasing in Your sight. I yield to Your correction. Purify my heart and my motives in this season so I emerge as a vessel fit for Your use. In Jesus's name I pray. Amen!

Chapter 11

OUR TRUE IDENTITY

As a person called to teach the body of Christ how to pray, I assumed I needed a strong and powerful voice in order to be effective. Boy, was I wrong. Even though I could only speak at a whisper, God caused multiple doors of opportunity to swing open. I was invited to pray at a prayer breakfast, speak at a women's conference, do an interview for a cover story for a Christian women's magazine, and lead weekly prayer conference calls as others listened in from all over the United States.

I didn't understand what God was doing. Why would He allow this? Didn't He know my voice needed to be healed before I continued the work He called me to?

Of course He knew. He also knew how ashamed I was of the sound of my voice.

Somewhere along the line, I had equated powerful prayer with a strong, powerful voice. I questioned why God was pushing me out of my literal and figurative comfort zones by having me lead others in prayer with an unstable, unpredictable tone that was sometimes raspy and cracking, or so soft that no one could hear me. When I told God that no one could hear me, He answered with a simple yet profound question that exposed the deeply rooted motives of my heart: *Who are you praying to, anyway? I can hear you just fine.*

In that moment, God reminded me that my prayers were to be directed to Him alone. Prayer was not designed to impress people or for me to gain the least amount of glory for myself. I knew I was not supposed to boast in how great and powerful I sounded when I prayed, but I had drifted away from that knowledge, allowing pride to creep in.

When Jesus first taught the disciples how to pray, He said, "When you pray, don't be like the hypocrites who love to pray publicly on street corners and in the synagogues where everyone can see them. I tell you the truth, that is all the reward they will ever get" (Matthew 6:5). I had lost sight of the true essence of what prayer is—a heartfelt conversation between God and man while offering up prayers and petitions, giving thanks, and interceding on behalf of others.

Despite the fact that I had one vocal cord and was unable to project, God heard the whispers of my soul. He heard and knew the cry of my heart before I uttered a single word.

It takes courage to press past our insecurities and shame, but it is necessary if we want to do the work God called us to do. I had to get over myself and what others thought of me. My attention needed to be on God, not on my voice or the fact that others were listening to me pray. This was another important lesson I learned while walking through the valley.

Valleys have a way of bringing us into alignment with our true identity while dispelling any and all lies we have believed about ourselves, God, and our God-given assignment.

Many of us can relate to the idea of battling thoughts of failure and defeat, especially when we are in a low place and being tested. The father of lies—Satan himself—is working overtime to whisper lies and accusations so we'll forget who we truly are in Christ. We doubt ourselves, and we wonder what we did wrong. We question if God really called us, or if we'll ever fulfill that call and make a real impact in the earth. As we see others move forward, we wonder if our life counts in the grand scheme of things.

In my low and humble state, physically limited by my voice, I was forced to depend on God every time I opened my mouth. That was when He began to teach me about my true identity, purify the motives of my heart, and reveal things I'd been unaware of.

I had prided myself in coming across like a true prayer warrior (whatever that is supposed to look and sound like). I wanted others to perceive me as a powerful woman of prayer, worthy of my call. After all, I was the author of the life-changing book, *Pray-ers Bear Fruit: Become a Person of Prayer*. If my prayers were going to be heard by others, shouldn't I make a good impression?

Not really. That didn't matter to God. It was my heart that concerned Him.

He cared more about my prayers flowing from a pure place than how my voice sounded. I learned another valuable lesson as well: my true identity is in Christ, not in my gifts or abilities, the way I look or sound, or how I come across to others.

Pride has no place in our lives as Christians. Especially if we plan to do anything to help advance God's kingdom. Our confidence must stem from God alone, not from ourselves or a fleshly attribute, experience, educational credential, or spiritual gift. Have you ever struggled to know your true identity?

- **Point to ponder: Our true identity can only be found in God. It has nothing to do with us or what we accomplish.**

Let's pray:

Father God, rid me of trying to establish my identity in anything other than You. Help me to discover who I am in Christ. Please give me a greater awareness of who I am in You and who You are in me. In Jesus's name I pray. Amen.

Chapter 12

THOUGH HE SLAY ME

M any people struggle to understand why God allows suffering. We have all experienced times when we find ourselves in the midst of trouble and don't understand why. Job was a man who endured a horrible season of testing.

Job's story is so difficult to process that there have been times I avoided reading it altogether—perhaps because I didn't want similar catastrophes to happen to me. What I find intriguing in the description of Job, however, is found in chapter 1. It reads, "There once was a man named Job who lived in the land of Uz. He was blameless—a man of complete integrity. He feared God and stayed away from evil. He was, in fact, the richest person in that entire area" (Job 1:1, 3).

Job was blameless, upright, and God-fearing, but he suffered tremendous lost. . . . He lost all of his children, cattle, workers, and many possessions. All that remained was Job's life and that of his wife. Upon hearing the news of all he had lost, "Job stood up and tore his robe in grief. Then he shaved his head and fell to the ground to worship" (v. 20). As if he hadn't suffered enough, Job's physical body was attacked (Job 2:7). Things got so bad that his wife asked him, "Are you still trying to maintain your integrity? Curse God and die" (v. 9). Even Job's three friends were miserable comforters. They misunderstood and misjudged his season of suffering.

Even so, Job stayed true to God, responding, "Should we accept only good things from the hand of God and never anything bad?" (v. 10).

Why do we struggle to trust God in the midst of trouble?

Have you ever been misjudged or misunderstood when you were suffering?

It's easy for those watching from the outside to attempt to label what we're going through and why.

Some biblical scholars believe Job's suffering was brought on by fear because Job was concerned that his children had sinned and cursed God in their hearts, so he constantly made burnt offerings to the Lord to cover what he thought they might have done. But the Bible tells us how Job entered into one of the darkest valley experiences ever written about in Scripture. It says, "One day the members of the heavenly court came to present themselves before the LORD, and the Accuser, Satan, came with them. 'Where have you come from?' the LORD asked Satan. Satan answered the LORD, 'I have been patrolling the earth, watching everything that's going on.' Then the LORD asked Satan, 'Have you noticed my servant Job?'" (Job 1:6–8).

I believe God trusted Job with the degree of suffering He allowed because He knew Job's heart toward Him was pure and upright. He knew Job would never curse Him. He knew Job would endure and come out on the other side of his trials victorious.

God knows us better than we know ourselves. Just when we think we cannot make it, or that what we're going through is beyond our ability to stand, God sees us as more than conquerors. He knows our hearts. He knows what we're made of because we are made in His image and in His likeness. In other words, we are like Him.

God allows us to pass through valleys because He can trust us with trouble.

One of the most fascinating things recorded in the book of Job is in chapters 38–41, when God begins to answer Job's questions concerning suffering. God doesn't respond the way we might expect. He answers Job's questions with more questions. He asks Job where he was when the earth was created. God asks Job one question after another until he realizes he knows nothing about anything and is speechless before God.

Suffering is God's business. He gives us the opportunity to discover more about Him—and ourselves—in the process. He grows us and increases our capacity for more.

> Then Job replied to the LORD: "I know that
> you can do anything, and no one can stop
> you. You asked, 'Who is this that questions
> my wisdom with such ignorance?' It is

I—and I was talking about things I knew nothing about, things far too wonderful for me. You said, 'Listen and I will speak! I have some questions for you, and you must answer them.' I had only heard about you before, but now I have seen you with my own eyes. I take back everything I said, and I sit in dust and ashes to show my repentance." ~Job 42:1–6

At the end of Job's season of suffering, he had to repent for questioning God and speaking of things he didn't understand—things too great for him to know while his heart and body were full of pain. After Job repented in dust and ashes, God told him to pray for his friends. The ones who analyzed and judged his situation. And in the end, God restored Job's losses and gave him twice as much as he had before.

The later days of Job's life were greater than the former days. God blessed Job and his wife, enabling them to have more children. Job lived one hundred and forty more years, long enough to see his children and grandchildren up to four generations (see Job 42). Job's suffering only lasted about nine months, but I'm sure its intense nature made it feel like a lifetime.

What lessons can we learn from Job's suffering that we can apply to our own lives?

- No matter what we go through, or what we've lost along the journey, we must stay true to God and trust Him through it all.

- We must pray for those who misjudge our situation, and forgive them.
- We must realize our suffering is not in vain.
- We cannot give up before we experience God's restoration in our lives.
- God wants to make it up to us for what we suffer. He desires to give us double for our trouble, so just like Job, our latter days are greater than our past.

What are some words you may have spoken in your time of trouble? Are there heart issues you need to repent of? Who may need your prayers and forgiveness?

- **Point to ponder: God trusts us with trouble. He knows we have what it takes to make it through.**

Prayer:

Father, You know me far better than I know myself. Thank You for trusting me and knowing the depths of my heart. I know You would never allow me to go through something that would destroy me in the process. I trust You to help me get through life's difficulties. Lord, when it's all said and done, please restore all that has been lost and give me double for the trouble I've endured. I pray this in Jesus's name. Amen.

Chapter 13

By Divine Providence

Over the past ten years, I've learned the value of seeking God's perspective on every situation. Whenever I find myself entering a valley, I search my heart to consider the reason. It's important to know if what I'm experiencing is coming from the Enemy, my own actions, or by God's divine providence.

Most of us are familiar with the biblical story about the valley of dry bones. Scripture tells us that the hand of the Lord came upon Ezekiel, and he was taken out in the Spirit and placed in the midst of a valley that was full of bones, and they were scattered all over the valley floor. God must have granted Ezekiel this out-of-body, supernatural experience for a divine purpose. It doesn't seem like this would be a welcomed experience, but it was necessary for Ezekiel to do the work of a prophet and obey God's calling. God then posed a question to Ezekiel.

> Then he asked me, "Son of man, can these bones become living people again?" "O Sovereign LORD," I replied, "you alone know the answer to that." Then he said to me,

> "Speak a prophetic message to these bones and say, 'Dry bones, listen to the word of the LORD! This is what the Sovereign LORD says: Look! I am going to put breath into you and make you live again!'" ~Ezekiel 37:3–5

When life looks beyond hope, God is ready to step in and breathe life into a dead situation. When God calls us to do a specific work, we may be required to walk through a valley to get what we need for our assignment. Sometimes God requires us to leave our comfortable or familiar surroundings so He can speak to us.

When we are busy living life as usual, our spiritual senses can become dull. Until we find ourselves in a valley, we lack spiritual foresight and the ability to be sensitive to God's voice. In the valley, however, God can speak to us one on one and show us things to come.

A Message of Hope

> Then he said to me, "Son of man, these bones represent the people of Israel. They are saying, 'We have become old, dry bones—all hope is gone. Our nation is finished.'"
> ~Ezekiel 37:11

Many of us know what it feels like to lose hope. Sometimes circumstances take us to such low places that it appears everything around us is lifeless and beyond being resurrected. When the Spirit of the Lord placed Ezekiel in the valley full of bones, the bones were dead, dry, and even disjointed, but they were not beyond hope.

God takes pleasure in showing off His power. He enjoys displaying the miraculous things He can do. After all, He is God. There is nothing too hard for Him. We have the privilege of coming to know and understand who He is and what He can do when we trust Him. When things look hopeless in our lives, God is looking for our faith. He's searching for those who really believe Him and are willing to trust Him even when they see no signs of life.

I'm sure Israel was unaware that God was about to send His prophet Ezekiel with a message of hope for what God was about to do in their lives. These people were not forgotten. They were about to live again and rise as a great army.

Neither has He forgotten you.

The greatest treasure to be gained by walking through a valley is the increase of our knowledge of God and what He can do.

After God brings you through trouble, you know Him from firsthand experience because you've walked with Him through the low places. When God breathes life into your dead situation, your testimony will tell the story that you know God personally and what He is able to accomplish.

God allowed Israel to come to the point of saying, "Our bones are dry, our hope is lost, and we ourselves are cut off" so they would really know Him. Until we are given the opportunity to parallel the highs of life against the low points, or experience the joys of life against the sorrows of death and watch God move on our behalf, we will not truly know Him. It's in the valley that trust and faith are born. The result is a rich, secure, and intimate relationship with our heavenly Father that nothing can shake.

Through His prophet, God spoke a word to people who were dead and without hope. At their lowest point, He promised to bring them up out of their graves and give them life.

If you are at a low point, don't lose hope. Hear the word of the Lord and apply it to your situation.

> Therefore, prophesy to them and say, "This is what the Sovereign LORD says: O my people, I will open your graves of exile and cause you to rise again. Then I will bring you back to the land of Israel. When this happens, O my people, you will know that I am the LORD. I will put my Spirit in you, and you will live again and return home to your own land."
> ~Ezekiel 37:12–14

We should never assess our situation based on the way it looks today. We must rise higher in our faith and listen for what God will speak to our heart. He will reveal what He desires to do in our lives in the days to come. God sees you. He has not forgotten you. We must be determined to come out of our low place knowing God better than we've ever known Him before. Do you feel as though your dreams have died or it's too late for the vision God gave you to come to pass? Does your life look hopeless? You have the power to prophesy God's Word over your life as often as necessary until change comes.

- **Point to ponder: It takes faith and hope to walk through a dark valley and speak life over dead and hopeless situations.**

Prayer:

> *Father God*, I need You to restore my hope. I know there is nothing too difficult for You. Help me believe for the impossible. In Jesus's name I pray. Amen.

Chapter 14

WALKING BY FAITH

Our faith can take us a long way. The greater our faith, the greater our ability to stand in tough times and believe God for the impossible. If our faith is small in the face of trouble, it's difficult to move forward. The Bible tells us, "If you faint in the day of adversity, your strength is small" (Proverbs 24:10 AMPC). Hard times don't give us an excuse to doubt God; they give us a reason to trust Him. We may doubt ourselves or others because, in our human weaknesses, we lack the power to change a situation. But we cannot afford to doubt God.

Jesus is the same yesterday, today, and forever (Hebrews 13:8). Therefore, He is consistent, reliable, and worthy of our trust. People can be fickle, unpredictable, and unreliable, but God is not. If you wonder if you can count on Him, just stop and look at His creation. The sun and moon are still right where God placed them on the day He spoke them into existence, and they are still doing what they are purposed to do. We never have to worry about God being inconsistent—in a bad mood one minute and a good one the next. We know His sun is there to light up each new day and His moon to brighten the earth by night. Above all, we can rely on God's Word. He promised, "Heaven and earth will pass away, but My words will by no means pass away" (Luke 21:33 NKJV).

Nothing forces us to exercise our faith walk quite like being in a valley. This is just a part of our Christian walk. It's a journey of faith. A valley requires believing in God and trusting in Him even when our senses fail us. We may see something different when we look around us. We may hear something contrary to God's Word with our ears. But we must continue to look to God. Walking with God and exercising our faith along the journey is the only way we can truly please Him.

> It was by faith that Enoch was taken up to heaven without dying—"he disappeared, because God took him." For before he was taken up, he was known as a person who pleased God. And it is impossible to please God without faith. Anyone who wants to come to him must believe that God exists and that he rewards those who sincerely seek him. ~Hebrews 11:5–6

When Your Faith Is on Trial

We must believe God against all odds, despite how things appear. When an unwelcome crisis arises and we feel pressured by our circumstances, we are tempted to panic or run and hide from the situation. The best thing we can possibly do is keep our eyes on Jesus, the

Author and Finisher of our faith. He knows how our story began, as well as how it is supposed to end. If we stay close to God and keep walking with Him, we will make it through anything.

I love Jesus's heart toward His disciples (that includes you and me). He always prepared them for what was going to happen next, but especially as the time of His death drew near. Jesus knew things were going to get intense and that Peter, in particular, would be pushed to his limit due to his relationship with Jesus. Remembering this point alone will bring some clarity to our situation and why we are tested.

"And the Lord said, 'Simon, Simon! Indeed, Satan has asked for you, that he may sift you as wheat. But I have prayed for you, that your faith should not fail'" (Luke 22:31–32 NKJV). Just like Jesus prayed for Simon Peter, He is interceding for us today. He doesn't want our faith to fail. He wants it to be what carries us through each valley.

When we face difficult situations and our backs are against the wall, our faith is what pleases the heart of God.

We can easily settle into our current situation, or simply give up as if God is incapable of caring for us in our time of need. But we must be convinced that He is the God of the turnaround. He specializes in impossible situations. Examples of men and women who walked by faith in the midst of impossibilities appear throughout Scripture. We see Moses's parents (Amram and Yochebed), who put him in a basket in the Nile river as an act of faith instead of allowing him to die along with all the other babies ordered to be killed. Moses was then found and cared for by the Egyptians and eventually used by God to deliver the Israelites from bondage. Abraham and Sarah gave birth to their son of promise despite their old age and the deadness of Sarah's womb. And the list goes on. Think of how different history would be without Moses and Abraham. They both had significant assignments to fulfill, but those assignments came with a price.

Wherever you find yourself today, remember it is not the end of your story. Keep walking by faith and not by sight. See how God will write your story and give you a glorious testimony that shows others what He can do.

Dump Your Doubts

In my opinion, one of the greatest Bible teachers on the subject of faith is the late Reverend Kenneth E. Hagin, founder of the Rhema Bible Training Center in Tulsa, Oklahoma. During the early years of my marriage, I read as many of his books on prayer, faith, the Holy Spirit, and growing up spiritually that I could get my hands on. I also had the wonderful privilege of hearing him teach at a conference.

Reverend Hagin taught an unforgettable message on what it means to walk by faith, and how doubt tries to creep in. He taught, "You can have doubt in your head, but not in your heart." He went on to explain that it is normal for believers to struggle with thoughts of doubt and defeat, but we cannot allow doubt to enter our hearts. In other words, we don't want to get to the point where we begin to doubt God. It is a dangerous place to be. We cannot expect to receive anything from the Lord if we doubt Him. I've used Brother Hagin's words as a gauge whenever doubt tries to enter my life.

The Enemy is quite masterful at using the power of suggestion to plant seeds of doubt in our minds. His ultimate plan is to convince us to meditate on his lies until we believe them in our hearts and accept them as facts. If we second guess what God has already told us, we will get ourselves in trouble by shifting our faith from God over to the Enemy. Let's look at two biblical examples of what this looks like.

Eve found herself in a predicament when Satan used the power of suggestion to deceive her.

> The serpent was the shrewdest of all the wild animals the LORD God had made. One day he asked the woman, "Did God really say you must not eat the fruit from any of the trees in the garden?" ~Genesis 3:1

Eve was doing fine—just minding her business—until the Enemy came along and cast a seed of doubt in her heart. We know doubt entered her heart because of her response—disobedience. Doubt caused Eve to do the one thing God had instructed her and Adam *not* to do. You can read the entire account in Genesis 3. Eve's story reminds us why it's important to watch and pray, to be alert and not ignorant of Satan's devices. As we casually go about our way, he is busy plotting and devising a plan against us. We must know God's Word and stick to it.

John the Baptist is our second example. When he found himself unjustly imprisoned for speaking the truth to Herod Antipas (the ruler of Galilee) about being married to his dead brother's wife, he doubted in his head but not in his heart. John probably wondered how this could happen to him when he was only doing the work he'd been called to do. He might have wondered where Jesus was and why He didn't come to get him out.

> John the Baptist, who was in prison, heard about all the things the Messiah was doing. So he sent his disciples to ask Jesus, "Are you the Messiah we've been expecting, or should we keep looking for someone else?" Jesus told them, "Go back to John and tell him what you have heard and seen—the blind see, the lame walk, those with leprosy are cured, the deaf hear, the dead are raised to life, and the Good News is being preached to the poor." And he added, "God blesses those who do not fall away because of me."
> ~Matthew 11:2–6

It's difficult to face circumstances that contradict the promises of God in our lives. It's not unusual to be bombarded with feelings of uncertainty and doubtful thoughts when we are in the midst of a valley, but the Word tells us, "Resist the devil, and he will flee from you" (James 4:7). We must resist the temptation to assess our situation and believe in how things appear instead of what God has said in His Word.

Has the Enemy been working overtime to fill your mind with lies and cause you to doubt God's love for you or what He has spoken to you concerning your future? Satan wouldn't waste his time attacking you in this area if you were not a threat to the kingdom of darkness. The Enemy is afraid of the impact your life will have in the days ahead. Satan knows you are destined to impact the world in the arena God has called you to, and in so doing you will damage the Enemy's kingdom and mess up his plans.

Remember, the voice of the Enemy is the voice of doubt.

If you are struggling with doubt and questioning if God has spoken to you or really called you to accomplish something significant for Him, it's not unusual.

We overcome doubtful thoughts by redirecting them back to God and His Word. Every lie of the Enemy can be replaced with verses of Scripture. We must meditate on God's Word both day and night and speak Scriptures aloud if we want to shift the atmosphere around us.

We must rehearse what God has spoken to us prior to entering into our season of testing. If God spoke it, He will make good on it. We cannot doubt Him in our hearts.

If you are currently in a valley and your faith is on trial, circumstances are only a test to see if you truly believe what God has said. God's plan for our lives will come to pass when we have faith in Him, not when we doubt Him. When doubts begin to mount up, simply speak to them and command them to go!

> I tell you the truth, you can say to this mountain, "May you be lifted up and thrown into the sea," and it will happen. But you must really believe it will happen and have no doubt in your heart. ~Mark 11:23

Hold On to Your Confidence

Anytime we're in the midst of a test or trial, the Enemy attacks our confidence. That's his job. He uses any means possible to cause us to doubt both God and ourselves. Even if he succeeds at getting us to doubt ourselves, we should never doubt God. He is faithful. We must hold on to His written and spoken Word no matter how bad things appear.

The longer we're in the valley, the more difficult it seems to maintain our confidence and know God will come through. Over the years, I've had plenty of practice with spiritual warfare, and because of it I've learned the patterns and tactics of the Enemy. He uses fear and doubt in his relentless attacks against us. But I've discovered that just when it seems like God has forgotten us or the Enemy is winning the war, our breakthrough is near.

So do not throw away this confident trust in the Lord. Remember the great reward it brings you. Patient endurance is what you need now, so that you will continue to do God's will. ~Hebrews 10:35–36

If we patiently endure, a great reward awaits us on the other side. When we stand on the Word and remain firm in our faith, we are doing the will of God and pleasing our Father in heaven. But if we succumb to fear and begin to doubt God, the Enemy will shortchange us of our blessings before they have a chance to manifest. I don't know about you, but I'd much rather fight the good fight of faith than give the devil even an ounce of glory.

And my righteous ones will live by faith. But I will take no pleasure in anyone who turns away. ~Hebrew 10:38

Keep your cool and stay poised, knowing God has your back. He will come through with a glorious reward, and you'll receive His promises to you. Our true confidence comes from who we are in Christ, not from ourselves.

- **Point to ponder: When we walk by faith with confidence, we please our heavenly Father.**

Prayer:

Heavenly Father, I look to You today. My help and confidence come from You. I repent for allowing doubt to creep in. Teach me to see things through the eyes of faith. I know You will walk with me through this season just like You have all others. I want to please You in every way possible as I stand in faith. Thank You for the rewards that come from patient endurance. In Jesus's name I pray. Amen!

Chapter 15

MAINTAINING PEACE

I learned that peace was a valuable gift from the Lord on the day I received a special gift from a woman I worked with. Inside a book of poetry written by Helen Steiner Rice, she wrote a note to encourage my aching heart and included what has become one of my favorite Scriptures, in which Jesus said, "I am leaving you with a gift—peace of mind and heart. And the peace I give is a gift the world cannot give. So don't be troubled or afraid" (John 14:27).

During my final days of high school, as I wrapped up my last few classes, worked a part time job, and tried to figure out what I wanted to do with my life, my dad lay dying in a hospital bed just one block up the road from my school. I remember leaving work each day and heading straight to the hospital to be at his bedside. I needed peace of mind and heart, and the only place I could find it was in God.

It's during the hard times that we realize the importance of our relationship with God. I'm so thankful I knew Him then, and I know Him even better now. I spent a lot of time cultivating my relationship with my heavenly Father. Even as I watched my dad slip away and felt angry at God for not healing him, somehow I still knew God was faithful and just. I rested in His sovereignty as best I could, and He was there to comfort me whenever I drew near.

Losing my dad was hard, but little did I know that just two years later, God would bless me with a father-in-law I would have the privilege of calling Dad for over thirty years. In many ways, my father-in-law reminded me of my dad. They resembled each other physically and were both sweet, kind, and gentle men. God heals our hearts and binds our wounds in the ways that are best for us.

Just because our hearts are hurting doesn't mean that God has left us. Even through my loneliest tearful hours, I sensed God's presence in a tangible way. He was only a whisper away.

Despite how dark your valley may seem, God wants you to maintain peace. It's His gift to you. Satan cannot take it away unless you relinquish it to him.

Overcoming Negative Thoughts

Sometimes maintaining peace is a day-by-day or hour-by-hour battle.

It seems strange to wage a fight over a gift received from God, but we must be willing to do whatever is necessary to stay in a peaceful place—no matter what is happening around us.

There were times when my marriage was in trouble and Satan launched a series of mental attacks. Terrible images would flash across my mind and cause me to feel sad to the point of tears. The Enemy was after my peace. I had to become very intentional about casting down imaginations and replacing those negative thoughts with Scriptures. The Word of God can dismantle any stronghold the devil attempts to build in our mind.

It's important to pay attention to our thoughts when we are in a valley. Satan uses the power of suggestion to attack our minds and pull us in the direction he wants us to go, but we don't have to take anything he dishes out. We have the power to redirect our thoughts as often as necessary. The Enemy can be relentless in his pursuit to make us feel depressed, discouraged, and defeated. Holding on to our peace can feel like a constant battle, but it can be done. Peace belongs to us as children of God.

> You will keep in perfect peace all who trust in you, all whose thoughts are fixed on you!
> ~Isaiah 26:3

- **Point to ponder: Peace is a gift from God. Don't let the devil take it away.**

Prayer:

> *Father,* I thank You for the gift of peace You have given me. Help me hold on to it and never let it go. Holy Spirit, remind me of God's words so I can declare them out loud and cast down every evil thought or imagination. I cover my mind with the precious blood of Jesus, shed for me long ago. I know

nothing can penetrate the blood of Your Son.
In Jesus's name I pray. Amen!

Chapter 16

HANDLING
THE UNEXPECTED

The events of our lives are no big surprise to God. But there are times when we are faced with unwelcome news that we are not expecting. As I was writing my first book, *Pray-ers Bear Fruit*, I was faced with a series of unexpected events, two of which I will share with you now.

My cousin Denise had been hospitalized and was about to be discharged, so I invited her to stay in our home until she felt strong enough to care for herself. She was young, single, and very independent. I was quite surprised when she took me up on my offer.

A couple of days before she arrived, I felt prompted to go and buy new bedding for our guest bedroom. I went shopping and found just the right items to make the room beautiful, warm, and inviting as I prepared for Denise's arrival.

Just a few days after Denise arrived, I prepared a Sunday dinner with all of her favorite dishes. The table was decorated with golden chargers, cloth napkins, and candles as if we were celebrating a special holiday.

We had good food and sweet fellowship together as Denise reminisced about our loved ones who had passed on. Our dads were brothers, both in heaven. Denise reflected on how our family always came together for weddings and funerals. We laughed a bit and talked about the good ole days when we were young.

After dinner Denise announced that it was time for her to go home. She said she had business to take care of and wanted to get back to her normal routine. Denise thanked me and my husband for spoiling her and told us she could get used to being treated so special.

At the time I didn't know why I felt so compelled to go about things the way I did. All I knew is my heart was full of love, compassion, and mercy to lavish it upon Denise. Just three short days after leaving our home, my dear Niecee, as I affectionately called her, went home to be with the Lord. I was heartbroken. Making the phone call to inform my aunt Gloria was the hardest call I've ever had to make. There was no easy way to tell her that her only daughter was gone.

The truth is this wasn't the first time Denise had been near death. As a kidney transplant recipient, for many years she was a true survivor and example of God's goodness and His grace. God blessed Denise with a great life, and she lived it to the fullest. She really knew how to have a good time. We had fun shopping together, eating out, and going to movies. She wasn't just a cousin; she was a close friend. We were not ready for Denise to leave us, but God saw fit to take her home. Denise loved the Lord and her family and friends. I know we will see her again.

Denise was such a kind and generous person. I found great comfort in knowing God granted me and my husband the privilege of caring for her in her final days on earth.

Emonne's Story

On Easter Sunday, after my husband and I returned home from a wonderful church service followed by a delicious meal, I decided to visit a friend. As I stood in her kitchen, I received an unexpected call that thrust me and my family into a valley.

I was happy to hear from our daughter, Emonne, but I wasn't prepared for what she had to tell me. "Mom, I'm coughing up blood."

I was a bit taken aback. I thought maybe she had a cold and was coughing up mucus tinged with blood, so I proceeded to ask questions about her symptoms and then told her to go to the hospital right away. The following morning, Emonne called from the hospital, her voice quivering. "Mom, they found a mass on my left lung, and they want to do surgery."

It's hard to describe the feelings that flooded my heart upon realizing that our only daughter, who lived hundreds of miles away, was in trouble. I wasn't there to hold her and tell her everything would be all right. My husband had just left for a business trip that morning, but when I called and gave him the news, he caught the next flight home. Later that evening, we drove to

Oklahoma to bring our daughter home. I was nervous just riding in the car, wondering if she could handle the trip. As I prayed and sought the Lord, He gave me wisdom to know what to do.

We had just moved to Texas and had no idea which doctor to call. After obtaining a referral from the emergency room physician who treated Emonne, we scheduled an appointment with a pulmonologist a few days later. After a brief consultation and exam, the specialist scheduled a test to assess the severity of Emonne's condition. We were told the test would take about twenty minutes, but within five to ten the doctor said, "If it walks like a duck and quacks like a duck, then it's a duck." At the time, I didn't realize what he was trying to say. I just knew Emonne needed surgery and her condition was very serious.

Emonne entered the deepest, darkest valley of her life. So did our entire family. She was in her junior year of college, only twenty years old at the time, and had never smoked a day in her life. The doctor was puzzled by Emonne's condition and told us he usually treated this type of condition in elderly patients. Our daughter was devastated. I asked myself, *How could this be happening?* and *Why now?*

Nothing pierces a mom's heart more than when her child is sick or in trouble and there is nothing she can do to spare them of pain, but I knew I had to be strong in faith. I had to reassure Emonne that everything was going to be all right.

The days leading up to the surgery were critical. Emonne's health rapidly declined. She was in the battle of her life, and that life seemed to be hanging in the balance. As I watched her suffer, I felt as though I would never smile again.

When we admitted Emonne to the hospital the night before her surgery, the surgeon came by to introduce himself and talk to the family. All Emonne wanted to know was how soon she could return to school. The doctor smiled, because he knew she had no idea of the recovery process ahead. He informed her that she would not be returning back to school to finish the semester, nor would she be able to take the mission trip she had planned. She would spend most of the summer recovering, in hopes of returning back to college in the fall.

When the time came for the nurses to take Emonne into surgery, a few friends gathered at the hospital to show their love and support for our girl. We all fought back tears as she was rolled into the operating room with her Bible resting on her chest—God's Word giving her peace and comfort in her most critical hour.

When the double doors to the surgery room swung shut and Emonne was no longer in sight, my knees buckled. My husband and my mom, who had traveled in from Michigan to be with us, held me up. I felt like Abraham must have felt as he laid his only son Isaac on the altar in obedience to God. I didn't know if our daughter would come back to us or not. I just didn't know.

The doctors discovered cancer in Emonne's body. They removed half of her left lung along with the surrounding lymph nodes. That day, we walked through the valley of the shadow of death, but God was with us.

As Emonne lay in my bed recovering over the summer, God spoke to my heart.

After this, then harvest.

I knew He was letting me know that even though we were walking through a deep, dark valley, our season was about to change. God always pays us back and gives us fruit when He allows us to suffer. I held on to His words as I encouraged Emonne about the bright future God had in store for her.

It's with a heart of thanksgiving that I can report that Emonne's life was spared. God was not finished with her yet. Out of one of the darkest times of her life, God brought forth abundant fruit. Emonne returned to finish her last year of college, and with hard work and determination, she graduated on schedule along with her friends.

I know that not every mom's story ends like mine. I have friends who have lost their children. As I prepared to attend Emonne's graduation, I had an encounter with another mom while at a nail salon. There I sat, full of joy, thinking about how blessed we were that Emonne was alive and well and about to walk across the stage and receive her college degree when, out of the corner of my eye, I noticed the woman getting her nails done in the chair next to me. She was crying. I asked her if she was okay, and she pulled a small picture frame from her purse. Inside the frame was a picture of a gorgeous young woman—her daughter—who had recently passed away from cancer.

My heart ached for this mom and the sorrow that filled her heart. I'm sure the depth of her pain was just as intense as the depth of my joy, and I was well aware that her story could have been my story. I don't understand why my daughter lived while this other mother had to bury hers. This encounter will forever be etched in my heart. The light on the other side of this woman's valley is that her daughter knew the Lord and, as Christians, they will see each other again in eternity. This is the promise we have in Christ.

> For our present troubles are small and won't last very long. Yet they produce for us a glory that vastly outweighs them and will last forever! ~2 Corinthians 4:17

Today, Emonne lives a full and vibrant life as a wife and a mother of two. She is an evangelist, author, and the founder of the Leave Your Beauty Mark foundation, a nonprofit organization that inspires young women to live a life of purpose and make their mark on the world. God is completing the work He had started in Emonne's life. He alone knows our times and seasons and the number of our days.

Another Mom's Story

As children of God, nothing occurs by mere happenstance. God has a way of taking that which is bad and fitting it into a plan for our good. As I was writing this book, I received an unexpected late-night phone call from a dear friend. I had just gone to bed, but I'm glad I decided to take the call. One of her sons had been hit by a car while riding his motorized scooter without a helmet. Frantically, she relayed the words she had just received from a total stranger who had been at the scene of the accident just minutes before. Victoria's beloved son was lying in a hospital, over two-thousand miles away, in a medically induced coma.

Victoria felt alone, helpless, and confused as she spent the night waiting on the doctors to run tests and assess the severity of her son's injuries. How could God allow this to happen? Why now? Victoria had just walked through one of the darkest seasons of her life, and now, just as things were beginning to look up, more bad news. Victoria and her son found themselves in the midst of a valley. It seemed like more than anyone could bear.

None of us know what we will encounter on any given day, especially when we are called according to God's purpose. To whom much is given, much is required. Like it or not, our faith will be tested. Walking through life's valleys requires us to walk by faith and not by sight and trust God despite our emotions or how the situation appears to our natural eyes.

Victoria had prayed for many years, asking God for some specific things concerning her family. When she began that journey, she knew she would have to pay a price to see the results. While some prayers were not answered the way she expected, God proved Himself faithful through it all. With her son's life hanging in the balance, however, Victoria's prayers seemed to be going in the opposite direction. All looked dark and hopeless.

But the story didn't end there.

While Victoria's son suffered from brain trauma, a fractured jaw and neck, broken teeth, and a knee injury, within a month's time she witnessed the hand of God work in a miraculous way. The injuries were not as bad or as life threatening as the doctors first suspected. What once looked like a long road to recovery began to turn around. Victoria's son miraculously improved by the day.

No matter how dark things may look, we must always leave room for the supernatural power of God to move on our behalf. God taught Victoria how to remain steady and consistent in Him, even when everything around her was unstable. She learned to take life one day at a time and not to be anxious about tomorrow. God revealed Himself to her as the great I AM. He showed Himself to be who she needed Him to be in a dark season of her life.

How do you respond when a crisis arises in your life? How do you handle unexpected news?

- **Point to ponder: When life looks dark and hopeless, God will be with us to comfort our hearts and see us through.**

Let's pray:

> *Heavenly Father*, I need You. Please give me the strength and courage to handle whatever comes my way. Help me to keep my eyes on You, and to put my complete faith, trust, and confidence in You. I know You will take care of all that concerns me. In Jesus's name I pray. Amen.

Chapter 17

THE POWER OF ALONENESS

When I was single, I thought marriage was the cure for loneliness. I thought it was impossible to have a lifelong companion and still feel alone. But I was wrong.

Loneliness is very real to the person who feels lonely. It's a mindset that often stems from the way we view life and the world around us. It can happen when our children grow up and go to school or move out of the house. It can happen when we lose loved ones. There are reasons we experience feelings of aloneness.

It is not unusual for loneliness and isolation to accompany us in a valley, especially if we are going through an individual test—something that impacts us alone. Some valleys include others, such as members of our family during times of loss. Other times, God allows us to go through something very personal, such as a crisis in our health or the severing of a close friendship or other relationship.

There are also times when God pulls us away from the crowd and the busyness of life to prepare us for the work He has called us to. If we plan to fulfill our purpose and complete the assignment we are given, we will face seasons of obscurity or anonymity.

Once we have come into awareness of our purpose, most of us want to be released into our destiny without spending time behind the scenes waiting for God to do a thorough work in us. But we must go through a process of preparation and refinement before God will use us. More importantly, we must know God intimately if we truly want to work for and with Him.

The way to know God is to spend time alone with Him, especially when we're in a low place where our heart is hurting, and we don't understand what is happening in our lives. Jesus often withdrew to a quiet place to be alone with the Father as He prepared for His earthly ministry. He knew when He needed to talk to the Father, and He sought to know the will of God.

God knows exactly why we're in a valley and what He wants to accomplish in us while we're there. In a season of isolation, fear and doubt try to grip our hearts. We may fear what will happen to us or someone we love. We may question if we will survive the crisis. But with God on our side, we cannot fail. He promised to never leave us or forsake us.

Satan is a master at magnifying our problems and pain to the degree that we feel like we will be consumed or destroyed by them. But if God allows us to enter into a valley, surely He will bring us out of it. God uses these seasons of testing to impart wisdom, understanding, and insight that we will carry with us as we move further along in our calling. He takes us through a valley to teach us valuable and life-changing lessons that, once mastered, empower us to rise to new heights and impact the world for God's glory.

In order to grasp what God is trying to impart to us, we must be still long enough to listen for His voice and come into the awareness of His abiding presence.

The moment we discover we are not alone, but that the Holy Spirit is in the valley with us, we are never the same. Jesus prayed to the Father, entreating the Holy Spirit to come and abide with us forever (John 14:16). Even if we willfully walk away from God, He will never leave us. As we journey through this Christian walk—even as we pass through valleys—the Holy Spirit is right alongside us, walking hand in hand with us. We don't need to fear, for the great Shepherd of our souls has a rod to protect us from the devourer and a staff to guide us along the path. When we put our trust in Him, God is well able to take care of us. We must choose to trust Him and rest in His presence, even when we cannot see or feel Him through our natural senses.

> For He [God] Himself has said, I will not in any way fail you *nor* give you up *nor* leave you without support. [I will] not, [I will] not, [I will] not in any degree leave you helpless *nor* forsake *nor* let [you] down (relax My hold on you)! [Assuredly not!] ~Hebrews 13:5 AMPC

The Art of Waiting and Resting

Resting in God requires us to trust His timing. God once instructed me to rest for a season, but I had no idea that season would last a full year. During that time, people asked what I was working on, or if I was writing or planning for a special event. All I could say was, "God has me in a season of rest."

Frustrated and restless, I was antsy to put my hands to something. I felt alone and isolated, as if I was being left behind while others moved forward in their assignments. It seemed like God was chastening me for something I did wrong, but He was allowing me time to rest and recover from a previous season that had been full of activity. A friend encouraged me when she said, "You better take advantage of this time and get plenty of rest. You will need it for the next season ahead."

She was right.

I finally took her advice and yielded to the will of God. I began to enjoy spending quality time in God's presence, being built up in the Word and in prayer.

Waiting can be difficult, especially when there are no signs of what we are believing for. After a while, we become anxious, wondering when our season will change. But every dream or promise that originates with God is one He is responsible for fulfilling. We are required to wait patiently on His timing. During our waiting times, we must ask ourselves if we would rather have a microwave meal or one that has been prepared in a slow cooker? If you consider how often most people use their microwaves versus their slow cookers when preparing meals, it seems most of us would choose the option that yields the quickest result, but that is not what is best or healthiest for us.

Something significant takes place inside us as we wait on God. When we refuse to rush through our season and we allow God to do a complete work in us, we come out better and stronger at the end of the process. God has made specific promises to those of us willing to wait on His timing:

> But those who trust in the LORD will find new strength. They will soar high on wings like eagles. They will run and not grow weary. They will walk and not faint. ~Isaiah 40:31

God promises us renewed strength. While we wait, we are empowered from on high with the ability to soar high like eagles. We can run our race and fulfill our purposes without growing weary and tired on the journey. We will make strides and not faint in the process of fulfilling our God-given assignments. As we wait upon the Lord, He equips us with all we need to be sustained on the next level.

Those who trust God realize it is far greater to wait than to rush the process and be ill-equipped for success and victory.

As we walk with God through the valleys of life, He graces us with endurance.

> Wait patiently for the LORD. Be brave and courageous. Yes, wait patiently for the LORD. ~Psalm 27:14

As you witness those around you moving forward and prospering on their journeys, waiting on God takes courage. This is why it is important to keep our eyes focused on God. Don't fret. He knows what He's doing. What God has for each of us is exclusively for us. No one can take it away. There is no need to compare our journey to someone else's. God wants to teach us things during times of aloneness, if we are willing to patiently wait in His presence.

Take a moment to close your eyes and imagine the Holy Spirit standing alongside you. As you wait upon the Lord, allow your heart to receive His comfort and the peace that surpasses all understanding.

- **Point to ponder: God uses aloneness to cultivate a deeper level of intimacy with Him and to teach us more about Him.**

Let's pray:

Father, thank You for never leaving me alone. Even when I feel lonely, I know You are still with me. Teach me how to rest in You and wait in Your presence. I want to experience more of You. Teach me whatever is necessary to prepare me for the future according to Your purpose and plan for my life. In Jesus's name I pray. Amen!

Chapter 18

SILENTLY LISTENING

God has blessed me with the gift of encouragement, but when others come to me for prayer
or counsel during a crisis, most tend to talk more than
they listen because they are full of anxiety and overwhelmed by their circumstances. I often find myself
waiting for them to take a breath so I can share what
God has placed on my heart for them.

This is the way we are with God. When we are heavily burdened, our words pour forth like water from a
faucet, offering momentary relief but no change. When
our talking finally ends, we may feel just as confused
and frustrated as we were at the beginning. Nothing is
resolved.

I used to do the same thing in times of trouble.
But as I began to grow up spiritually by cultivating an
intimate relationship with God through daily prayer, I
stopped turning to people and, instead, went straight
to God. People couldn't help me like God could. Still,
I had to train myself to sit still and quiet in God's presence, and listen long enough to hear His voice speaking
gently to my heart. Sometimes He gave me a simple

impression or a word that offered me direction and insight into my situation. Other times He provided a strategy or step that would lead me into victory.

> My sheep listen to my voice; I know them, and they follow me. ~John 10:27

The greatest and most exciting part of prayer is listening with expectancy for God to speak. When we're overwhelmed by our circumstances, it becomes easier to run to God and tell Him all about our troubles. But we need to listen for His direction and instruction. God already knows what weighs heavily on our hearts. He knows how these things affect our soul (mind, will, and emotions). But it is important to stop, take a deep breath, and cease from fretting and being anxious. We must force ourselves to be still long enough to hear what God has to say.

> Let all that I am wait quietly before God, for my hope is in him. ~Psalm 62:5

It's difficult to be quiet and still when everything around us is in turmoil, but it is the most important thing we can train ourselves to do—not only when we're in a valley, but whenever we spend time in prayer. Taking time to be still and quiet in God's presence positions us to hear His voice.

When we're in a low place, we must keep God's Word nearby, along with a notebook or journal. We must listen with expectancy to hear God speak to our heart. This shows God we are waiting to hear what He has to say.

If you begin the practice of waiting in His presence and don't hear anything from Him right away, don't be discouraged. Just keep practicing being still, listening, and waiting expectantly before God each day. He always speaks to those who take time to listen.

When was the last time you truly quieted yourself before God to listen?

Now is the perfect time to hear from the Lord. If you're able, take a moment and go to a quiet place. Make yourself comfortable. Play your favorite worship music to set the atmosphere and welcome the presence of God. Close your eyes and simply listen.

Be sure to write down whatever God speaks to your heart as well as any impressions (ideas, thoughts, or intuitions) that come to your heart so you can refer back to them. Ask the Lord to reveal the meaning or significance of what He shows you.

- **Point to ponder: In the valley, it's more important to listen than to speak.**

Let's pray a simple prayer:

Speak, Lord. I'm listening.

Chapter 19

KNOWING GOD AND DOING GOD'S WILL

I f we plan to do anything for God, we must first get to know Him. We must want Him to know us and claim us as His own. This requires us to know His will and what He desires to accomplish in the earth realm before we ever step out to accomplish anything for Him.

It would be terrible to attempt to build a ministry or business under the pretense that we're doing it for the Lord when He has no claim to it—or even worse, no claim to us. The Bible tells us, "For many are called, but few are chosen" (Matthew 22:14). We want to be God's chosen vessels of honor, without selfish or impure motives, with the purpose that all we do is for the advancement of God's kingdom.

Jesus said, "Not everyone who says to Me, 'Lord, Lord,' shall enter the kingdom of heaven, but he who does the will of My Father in heaven" (Matthew 7:21 NKJV). He didn't say a few people will say, "Lord, Lord, we did these things in Your name." He said *many* will speak those words. Do we want to be among the elite who truly know God through a real relationship with

Him and are doing His will? Or do we want to be a part of the crowd—the "many"—who don't know Him at all?

Valleys are designed a be a place of God-discovery. Life's challenges afford us opportunities to draw nearer to God. The nearer we are, and the more time we spend with Him, the more we will begin to know Him. When we come to the place where all we can do is turn our attention toward God and seek His face, we will begin to increase in our knowledge of Him.

It's that simple. Difficult seasons exist to bring us to the realization that we cannot live without being in close fellowship with God. Most people who walk closely with the Lord do so because they became desperate to know God and hear His voice in their darkest hours.

> On judgment day many will say to me, "Lord! Lord! We prophesied in your name and cast out demons in your name and performed many miracles in your name." But I will reply, "I never knew you. Get away from me, you who break God's laws.'   ~Matthew 7:22–23

There was a time when I felt puzzled and filled with godly fear and reverence over the thought of someone having the power to cast out demons and do many wonders in Jesus's name, only to hear, "Depart from me, for I never knew you." He doesn't say, "I once knew you, but you walked away from Me." He says, "I *never* knew you!"

Never means never. That's a frightening and sobering thought—one that beckons us to take a closer look at our relationship with God and examine the motives behind everything we think we are doing for Him.

When we reach the point where our personal goals and agendas become secondary to the will of God, we have arrived at the right place. Jesus taught His disciples to pray for God's kingdom to come and His will to be done on earth as it is in heaven. When we move beyond our selfish pursuits and desires for advancement and success—when we no longer strive to build our personal platforms—*then* we are truly living to do the will of God. I truly believe God brings increase to our lives as He sees fit.

To know God and do His will must be our highest pursuit and greatest desire.

The Gift of Knowing Him

When I look at where I am today, I stand in awe of God. Only He knows the depths of the work He has accomplished in my life and heart. I have not arrived at a place of perfection, and I will not become all I was created to be until Jesus returns or takes me home to meet Him face to face, but I've come a mighty long way.

I wish I had room to tell you all that God has done and brought me through, but that is not the focus of this book. When I think about my spiritual growth and maturity, and the level of intimacy I share with God, I realize I've arrived at this place by way of many valleys.

I didn't like what I had to go through when I was experiencing it, but I wouldn't trade my valley experiences because of what they yielded in my life.

Transformation takes place in the lowest seasons of our lives, when we draw near to God and refuse to let Him go.

When storms arise, we are presented with a choice. We can either use the opportunity to come to know God more intimately in a place of total surrender, or we can turn to other things as coping mechanisms to numb our pain or discomfort. The latter never works.

"And this is eternal life, that they may know You, the only true God, and Jesus Christ whom You have sent" (John 17:3 NKJV). Jesus came to give us life more abundantly. He gave His life that we could have eternal life. He came that we could know God and have relationship with Him. Imagine how differently we would handle the valleys we encounter if we looked at them through the lens of God's great love for us.

> This is what the LORD says: "Don't let the wise boast in their wisdom, or the powerful boast in their power, or the rich boast in their riches. But those who wish to boast should boast in this alone: that they truly know me and understand that I am the LORD who demonstrates unfailing love and who brings justice and righteousness to the earth, and that I delight in these things. I, the LORD, have spoken!" ~Jeremiah 9:23–24

God allows us to encounter trouble so we'll turn our attention toward Him. This is how He reveals Himself to us. Every valley allows us to experience another facet of God, leaving us in awe of Him and how much He loves us. He is not concerned about how smart we are, our educational endeavors, or what we have accomplished. He is not concerned about our fame, popularity, or the wealth we may acquire on this earth. What's most important to God is that we know Him—that we love Him with our whole hearts and love others the way we love ourselves.

- **Point to ponder: Our greatest quest in life is to know God and do His will.**

Pray this prayer with me:

Father God, I want to know You. I know whatever the cost or level of suffering You allow me to endure to truly know You and do Your will, and hear You say, "Well done, my good and faithful servant" is well worth the journey. In Jesus's name I pray. Amen!

Chapter 20

A THANKFUL HEART

It can be difficult to feel an overwhelming sense of gratitude and thanksgiving when you're going through a trial. It takes quietness before God and reflecting on what He has already done for gratitude to spring forth from the depths of your heart. You may wonder how one can be thankful for something bad that has happened, but God has a way of bringing good from the bad things in our lives.

As we gain an understanding of the place we're in, we can use our difficulty as a driving force to propel us into our purpose. But if we allow what we're going through to cause us to become negative or ungrateful, Satan has succeeded in his strategic plan against us.

The situations of life either make us or break us. If the Enemy has his way, he will break us, but if God has His way in our lives, He will make us what and who we were destined to be. The Bible tells us to "Rejoice always, pray without ceasing, in everything give thanks; for this is the will of God in Christ Jesus for you" (1 Thessalonians 5:16–18 NKJV).

Giving thanks in the good times as well as the bad empowers us to overcome anything that comes our way.

Even when we don't feel like we have anything to be thankful for, we do. There is always a reason to give God praise, but we need our eyes to be opened to see God's abundant blessings all around us. We must train ourselves to praise God through our pain. This is what it means to offer up the sacrifice of praise.

Life can be tough, but God is always good. If we look hard enough, we will see His goodness. The fact that you're alive and able to read this book is due to God's goodness. If you're facing a difficult situation, you can still find a reason to give thanks to God. It's His will for your life.

A thankful heart always results in something good, and it will turn any situation around. If we start our day in thanksgiving, we can shift a negative environment into something positive and full of life—just by being thankful.

Let's stop right now and take a moment to exercise our gratitude.

Make a list of the good things God has done for you over the past few days. It may not seem possible as you begin writing, but I guarantee your list will be longer than you anticipate. They don't have to be big things. Start with the small and watch your list grow . . . and keep on growing. We can never beat God's acts of love and kindness in our lives. If He never does another thing for us—if He never answers another of our prayers—He has done enough by sending Jesus to earth to save us.

- **Point to ponder: God deserves our thanks even in times of trouble. Thanksgiving is the vehicle that propels us forward to brighter days ahead.**

Let's pray:

Father God, I repent of the times I've been ungrateful and, as a result, have forgotten to stop and say, *Thank You, Lord, for the marvelous things You've done.* Please open my eyes to see Your goodness and lovingkindness all around me. Help me to recognize the things You have already done for me, and thank You in advance for what's to come. I love You and I give You the highest praise. In Jesus's name I pray. Amen!

Chapter 21

THE POWER OF
OUR TESTIMONY

God never allows us to go through a test without gaining a testimony, but we must have the courage and willingness to endure what comes our way. As I walked through my four-year journey with vocal cord paralysis, I didn't realize God was establishing a testimony for me to share in this book.

As I shared in a previous chapter, soon after the surgery, when I could barely lift my voice above a whisper, God began to open doors for me to speak. On one occasion, when I was at a conference in Miami to teach a writing workshop, one of the guest speakers called me forward during a general session and spoke a prophetic word over my life. I won't share the details, but in essence I was told that God would begin to use my voice to speak prophetically. It was a powerful word that left me humbled. I didn't understand how or why God could use me with my voice in such a terrible state, but He was going to use me in a special way.

The very next morning, before I could relish in the prophecy spoken over my life, I received a call from a friend who was in trouble. Her husband of over forty years had announced to her that he was filing for divorce. This immediately thrust me into a new assignment. I felt ready to move forward with a newfound zeal and excitement, but I didn't have the heart to abandon my friend at such a critical time in her life. It was as if she had fallen down and I was the only one willing to turn back to help her get back up again.

God didn't waste any of that time. From one phone call to the next, day after day after day and year after year until her divorce was final, I yielded my little voice and its limitations and allowed God to use me.

I counseled, encouraged, interceded, and prophesied as the Holy Spirit gave me the words, until I felt I had nothing left to give. On many occasions I felt exhausted. My throat hurt. I just wanted to rest. This was one of the toughest assignments I've ever endured. I wanted to quit a thousand times and just walk away. I didn't understand why God was pushing me beyond what I thought I could bear.

The exercising of my vocal cords can be likened to physical therapy or being worked out by a trainer. It hurts. It's not fun. I didn't feel like using my voice, but it was necessary.

Oftentimes we are pushed beyond our limits to develop strength and endurance of mind, body, and spirit that will take us to new levels. It took every ounce of faith for me to keep going on, but I couldn't give up.

My healing process was quite unique.

While I was busy helping someone who could barely help herself, God was in the process of healing me. When my thyroid was dysfunctional, I was also anemic, literally dragging through life because I had no energy, and I gained about twenty pounds. Several months following my surgery, God led me to park my car near a gym one day and go in. But it wasn't just any old gym. It was a personal training facility.

My son, a professional athlete, was accustomed to working with professional trainers. I had never hired someone to help me exercise. I had to get my fight back, but I was willing to do everything within my power to regain my health and to get back into shape. I was desperate for change! I began to work out three days a week with the help of a trainer and walk five to six days a week on my own. While I was doing what I could do to get better, God did what only He could do.

During this journey, when I was in church surrounded by thousands of people who were freely singing and worshiping God, I could barely lift my voice to sing. But I learned true worship is a heart-to-heart experience. One morning, when I was singing and worshiping the Lord as I got dressed for the day, I noticed I was singing in the soprano range—something I hadn't done in four years.

To my utter amazement, God restored my voice!

My heart filled with joy and thanksgiving over what He suddenly and unexpectedly did. From that day forward, I've sung as loudly and as freely as I desired, with tears of joy for what the Lord has done.

I scheduled an appointment to see my ENT doctor so he could look at my vocal cords one more time.

Surprisingly enough, my right vocal cord was still not moving, yet I could project my voice with only one of my vocal cords functioning. It's truly a miracle!

Now that I'm on the other side of that lengthy valley full of challenges and uncertainty, I've learned this:

The true beauty that emerges from life's valleys is the testimony gained for God's glory.

Our testimonies show us, as well as others, what God can do, and that if He did it for us, He can do it for them too. A testimony strengthens and encourages the hearer. It gives us the courage to handle the challenges that come our way as we are reminded of what God has done in times past.

Early one morning, during a time of prayer, the Lord spoke to my heart: *A testimony is forged through the fires of affliction.* I stopped to ponder those words.

To be forged means to be formed by pressing or hammering, with or without heat; it means to be made into a desired shape. Through the tests we endure as we walk through life's valleys, our testimony is formed or takes shape.

One definition of *affliction* is a cause of persistent pain or distress. It is also the state of being afflicted by something that causes suffering. This is what we endure through life's valleys in order to gain a testimony.

The word tells us, "Many are the afflictions of the righteous, But the LORD delivers him out of them all" (Psalm 34:19 NKJV). As Christians, we can expect to suffer and endure affliction on our journey as we walk with the Lord, But He will surely deliver us and give us testimonies worthy of sharing with the world. Our testimonies are proof of God's ability and power to rescue us from destruction and give us an abundant life.

A testimony is our personal account of how we encounter Jesus. It is our story for His glory.

No one can argue with us about whether or not our testimonies are true. No one can take them away from us. Our lives are the living proof of God's goodness. There is really no difference between our testimonies and those we read in Scripture. Each of us has our own personal story of what happened to us when we encountered God (Father, Son, and Spirit).

Throughout the Gospels, men and women were anxious to run and tell others what Jesus had done for them. Our response should be the same. When God does His work in our lives, we cannot keep it to ourselves. We must share it with others and, in the process, God receives the glory. Our journeys through life's valleys may seem long, and at times unbearable, but we must keep moving forward with the Lord.

> For our present troubles are small and won't last very long. Yet they produce for us a glory that vastly outweighs them and will last forever! So we don't look at the troubles we can see now; rather, we fix our gaze on things that cannot be seen. For the things we see now will soon be gone, but the things we cannot see will last forever. ~2 Corinthians 4:17–18

Trouble won't last always. Even when God allows us to suffer for His name's sake, it is working in us a greater degree of glory and preparing us for eternity. There will come a day when our adversary, the devil, will wish he had never looked our way. Even when it seems like he is winning the war and we're about to go under, we need to remember things are not as they appear. God will step in and deliver us. In Him, we always have the victory!

We already know the end of our story. The Bible says, "And they overcame him by the blood of the Lamb and by the word of their testimony, and they did not love their lives to the death" (Revelation 12:11 NKJV).

I wouldn't have had the privilege of writing this book had I not victoriously walked through life's valleys with the Lord. Yes, it was hard. Many times, I did not understand what God was doing in my life, and some valleys lasted so long that I thought I would never get through them. But I did. God always graciously takes me through to the other side. I know He will do the same for you. God shows no favoritism.

The day God spoke *Meet Me in the valley* to my heart, I knew He had something wonderful in store. But I had no idea this book was a part of His plan. Looking back, I wouldn't trade my life experiences, including the valleys, because of what I gained along the way. Today I know God more intimately, I have a greater awareness of who I am in Christ, and I know the true reason I do the work I've been called to do. I'm thankful for the place God has brought me to. It's all for His glory.

> Yes, everything else is worthless when compared with the infinite value of knowing Christ Jesus my Lord. For his sake I have discarded everything else, counting it all as garbage, so that I could gain Christ and become one with him. ~Philippians 3:8–9

In this life, not every day will be easy or perfect. We will endure seasons of suffering. But if we gain the knowledge of Christ in the process, it's well worth it. God is always faithful to His children. He will see us through every circumstance we encounter as we place our trust in Him.

Whether my days on earth are good or not-so-good, I'm thankful to be gaining a greater knowledge of the true and living God. I've learned to trust Him more because of what I've been through, and I love Him just the same.

What about you? What is your story for God's glory? What have you gained from the valleys God has allowed you to walk through?

- **Point to ponder: The true beauty that emerges from life's valleys are the testimonies we gain for God's glory.**

My closing prayer for you:

Father God, I pray for the person reading this book. I ask You to draw them closer to You. Let the eyes of their understanding be enlightened as they open their heart to whatever You desire to teach them along life's journey. Whether they find themselves on top of the most breathtaking mountain, or they are called to walk through the deepest valley, I pray they will discover the greatest joy and contentment in knowing You intimately, God, and bringing You glory. Amen!

Thank you for purchasing this book and taking time to read it. It was a true labor of love. If you were blessed by the words in this book, please do me a favor and share it with your friends and loved ones. Below, I've listed a few ways you can help me spread the word:

Write a review on Amazon.
Like my Facebook page and share my posts at the link below:
https://www.facebook.com/AuthorKathyRGreen
Follow me on social media via KathyRGreen, Twitter, Instagram, and YouTube @KathyRGreen.
Post your favorite quotes from the book via social media.

Contact me and share how this book has blessed you.

Mailing Address:
KRG Publications, LLC
P.O. Box 271598
Flower Mound, TX 75027-1598

Website: KathyRGreen.com/contact

ORDER INFORMATION

To order additional copies of this book, please visit
www.redemption-press.com.
Also available on Amazon.com and BarnesandNoble.com
Or by calling toll free 1-844-2REDEEM.